Congratulations

CW01072856

By purchasing an original o~~~~ encouraging African writers. If you suspect it has been copied or pirated, please contact the publishers:

- info@storymojaafrica.co.ke
- Blog: http://storymojaafrica.wordpress.com
- Website: www.storymojaafrica.co.ke
- Or write to:
  Storymoja
  P.O. Box 264-00606
  Sarit Centre
  Nairobi, Kenya

Storymoja books are published by No Boundaries Ltd., an ethical, indigenous company formed by a collective of writers committed to promoting African writing of a world class standard.

© Sunny Bindra
First published in March 2010 as a Storymoja imprint by No Boundaries Ltd., P.O. Box 264-00606, Sarit Centre, Nairobi, Kenya

ISBN 978-9966-001-13-9

Printed and bound at Thomson Press (India) Ltd

DEDICATION

**To my peculiar son, Vivek, who
finds even more joy in absurdity
than I do.**

THE
PECULIAR
KENYAN

SUNNY BINDRA

What others have said about Sunny Bindra's writing
(From: www.sunwords.com)

"As an avid reader, I have come across few who write as well as this... simply, creatively, with a tinge of sarcasm."
Patricia Mambo (Nairobi, Kenya)

"One of the finest and most refined journalists of our times... a rare pedigree!"
Eric Mutunga (Nairobi, Kenya)

"A cut above the best. A true sage."
Kenn Munyeki (Male, Maldives)

"I am a self-confessed Bindraholic!"
Elvis Biwott (Bomet, Kenya)

"Sunny is a portable library."
Ken Nyaga (Naivasha, Kenya)

"One of our best writers who continually provokes our thoughts."
Pinaken Patel (Ontario, Canada)

"Humour loaded with powerful messages. You make my Sundays!"
Beliah Bashabe (Kampala, Uganda)

"Absolutely delicious material."
Wangui Munyua (Nairobi, Kenya)

"Truly African, you touch on the very issues that we encounter daily here in Africa."
Kamau Gatheru (Beira, Mozambique)

"Somebody show me a writer better than Bindra. You make me buy the SUNDAY NATION."
Yusuf Mohamed (Watamu, Kenya)

"The most important writer in Kenya."
Steve Peifer (Kijabe, Kenya)

CONTENTS

Foreword

"Kenyans have very peculiar calling habits."

I know for sure I never did say those words myself, but over the years have come to accept their attribution to me. However, I have also come to accept that actually I was "right": Kenyans are indeed a peculiar bunch of people! Who for example would apply for "free" credit of KShs 50 when you actually never needed it? The answer is the over 1.7 million people on day one when we launched the product, "Okoa Jahazi!"

Sunny Bindra strikes a chord with his writings every Sunday, and now in this new book. He writes with humour yet with wry honesty asking serious questions about ourselves and our behaviour.

Reading this book is like looking in the mirror every morning. This is our nation, our character, our strengths and our weaknesses. We are indeed (to be generous) a peculiar lot. We sing and dance with our fellow Kenyans one minute, and then despise and even kill them the next. We stand together as "One Nation" against interfering foreigners (especially those colonialists) and then stand divided against our neighbours because their forefathers come from another part of our country.

I read this book, and indeed the Sunday columns from which it has emerged, with pleasure, relishing the sense of comedy being played out. Sometimes the commentary is sad -- but I always recognise that this is, and was, and will be an honest view of Kenyans (and yes, even of me).

We are peculiar but we are also lovable and hardworking, diligent and hospitable. But please don't ALL call at 8 o'clock every night (including Saturdays and Sundays)...

Michael Joseph, CEO, Safaricom

Introduction

Many moons ago (as we say in Kenya), Michael Joseph, CEO of the mobile-phone company Safaricom, said something that caused consternation. Responding to complaints about network congestion, Mr. Joseph was reported to have said the problem was partly caused by Kenyans' "peculiar calling habits." Kenyans had some unusual tendencies, suggested the business leader, when it came to using their mobile phones, such as everyone using their phones simultaneously after finishing work on a Friday, or calling free numbers incessantly.

Although Mr. Joseph thinks he was misunderstood (see Foreword), the country's chattering classes responded in outrage to this phrase, blasting the CEO for being insensitive. Kenyans did not like the idea of being "peculiar" at all.

Safaricom went on to become the region's largest and most profitable company, suggesting Michael Joseph knew what he was talking about, and suggesting that he used his understanding of Kenyans' peculiarities to drive the dramatic growth of his company.

Mr. Joseph has not used the word "peculiar" in public again, but I certainly have. From early 2003 I have been writing "A Sunny Day", a weekly column in the *Sunday Nation*, the region's leading newspaper. The column is a weekly polemic against all that is bad in Kenya and, less frequently, a celebration of all that is good. If there's one thing I can confirm after a lifetime of watching my fellow Kenyans and recording their behaviour, it is this: we are indeed peculiar. VERY peculiar. The odd, the strange, the eccentric and the outright bizarre are often very much the norm here. This has given me access to a huge pool of material for my column. Over the years, I have taken great pleasure in placing my tongue firmly in my cheek and writing about peculiar Kenyans. That includes most of us.

Or does it? So you think you're not one of these peculiar Kenyans? If so, immediately jump to the quiz on page 15 for proof of how peculiar you are...

Many of our leaders rob us blind and don't even pretend otherwise - but aren't you one of those who march to the polls every few years and re-elect them with gusto? You observe that top public servants are sometimes amongst the richest people in the country - but have you ever stopped to ask why? You might do so in private - but do you ever raise the question publicly? As a voter, you are most peculiar.

Being a member of your tribe has probably never given you any personal benefit - not once. But you line up behind tribal chieftains, who use your votes to enrich themselves. When a text message joke belittling members of another tribe arrives on your phone, what do you do? Laugh loudly before forwarding it to several friends, taking care not to inadvertently send it to other colleagues who belong to the tribe being insulted. You call yourself a Kenyan, but to which Kenya do you belong? As a citizen you are most peculiar.

As a consumer, you get service that is mediocre at best and downright insulting at worst - but do you ever complain, or withdraw your business? As a customer, you are most peculiar.

On the roads, you watch your fellow Kenyans turn into homicidal maniacs and reckless chancers. You meekly allow them to cut in front of you and bully you. In buses and matatus, you sit quietly as the drivers take you to hell and back. When you get behind the wheel yourself, you do the same. As a road-user, you are most peculiar.

Scan this sample menu of our daily headlines:

Minister refuses to resign after being implicated in massive scam, blames his political opponents.

Another building collapses, killing six.

Bus rams truck on highway, 35 feared dead.

Villagers scooping fuel from overturned tanker burn to death after explosion.

Foreign development partners issue new ultimatum.

Three wives in court over dead MP's estate.

We ingest this shocking menu every day, and then carry on as though nothing has happened. Business as usual.

What about your personal habits? When you say, "see you at two o'clock," don't you mean, "see you sometime in the afternoon - maybe?" Won't you be blaming the traffic when you finally arrive? At your workplace, how much office stationery do you cart off home, without for a moment thinking you're doing anything wrong? How much peculiar parenting do you do, having kids you have no hope of supporting and leaving housemaids to raise them?

My aim here is not to focus on just the grim and the miserable. Peculiarity is also a cause for celebration, and I want to celebrate the Peculiar Kenyan in this collection. Over the years, I have

11

poked gentle and not-so-gentle fun at my fellow Kenyans (and myself). It is those pieces, written with a light touch and a big smile, that I have gathered here in this handy volume.

I celebrate those Kenyans who wake up smiling and go to bed smiling, regardless of what happens in between. I celebrate the resilience of a people who can come through the toughest of times and still be optimistic that the future is bright. At the time of writing this, the *Nation* has just released a survey that shows the majority of Kenyans are happy in 2009. This at a time when we are still nursing the wounds of 2008's post-election violence; when the world around us is in deep recession; when we are in the middle of the worst drought of recent times, and famine stalks the land; and when our political leadership is morally bankrupt. To be happy at a time like this demonstrates startling resilience. This is one peculiarity the rest of the world needs to study!

In fact, our peculiarities may be what unite us. At a time when our nationhood is in peril and we are retreating back into ethnic kingdoms, let us come out and celebrate the fact that whether we emerge from lakes, mountains or oceans, we are uniformly peculiar! Anyone looking for a means of uniting Kenyans need look no further than our national eccentricities. Perhaps we have uncovered a national asset...

In the articles you will find here, I have used the weaponry of humour to address these issues. Sometimes it just isn't worth being too sanctimonious about things. You can often achieve more by ridiculing people rather than jumping up and down in anger.

I would be delighted to find you laughing long and hard as you read these pieces. But not too long. I may be deploying humour, but my intent is altogether serious. I am not being smug or superior by asking you to laugh at Kenyans. In 2003, I asked what a real Kenyan was:

> A Kenyan...is not just someone born in this country or living in it. A Kenyan is not just someone with a piece of paper bestowing nationality. A Kenyan is not just someone wearing the fake smile of patriotism and speaking the insincere words of nationalism. A Kenyan is someone who loves Kenya - as a place and a set of peoples - with a great passion. A Kenyan is someone who acts in the interest of all Kenyans. A Kenyan is a person who unites people regardless of ethnicity or tribe. A Kenyan is a person who thinks and acts outside his little box of tribe, religion, skin colour, or social class.

We are facing a great shortage of such persons in this country, and it is costing us dearly.

"A real patriot," said William Vaughan "is the fellow who gets a parking ticket and rejoices that the system works." Under that definition, there are precious few patriots around.

Behind each idiosyncrasy unearthed in the pages that follow lies a national issue. Poverty and desperation cause many of the behaviour patterns observed across Kenya. Colonial conditioning continues to shape habits and norms, 45 years later. So we should laugh, certainly: laughter is great *dawa*. But we must also stop to reflect, to understand, and finally act.

The articles collected here have been updated and edited from the original *Sunday Nation* pieces. I have enjoyed revisiting them, and I hope you will too.

Sunny Bindra
January 2010

CHAPTER ONE
How Kenyan Are You?

Another way to ask this question: How peculiar are you? The more 'Kenyan' you are, the more peculiar you are likely to be and vice versa. And I can prove this by using a favourite device, the quiz. The idea being, you check your "Kenyan-ness" or level of peculiarity by scoring yourself on a scale I provide.

I enjoy constructing these tests, but some readers take them way too seriously, writing to me to tell me their marks! Is this perhaps a symptom of our national preoccupation with examinations? We seem to be more concerned with the marks scored than with what the questions meant...

The first test of "Kenyan-ness" follows. More quizzes are found in later sections.

How Kenyan Are You?
(Part 1)

1. **When you vote for an MP, you vote for:**

    a. The candidate with the experience, skills and nature to bring development to your constituency

    b. The candidate with the loudest voice and the biggest car

    c. The candidate who gives you the biggest bribe

2. **When you vote for a political party, you vote for:**

a. The party with the best thought-out manifesto and the most credible policies to attack poverty in the country

b. The party with the most money, posters, T-shirts, advertisements and helicopters

c. The party that most of your fellow tribes-people vote for

3. **A political rally is being organised in your hometown this weekend. You:**

a. Ignore it and do something productive for your family or community instead

b. Check the list of speakers and decide to attend if someone of substance is speaking

c. Attend for sure, sit in the hot sun and/or cold rain for at least five hours, and clap and cheer with glee when you hear a speaker hurl abuse at other politicians

4. **When you can afford a car, you buy:**

a. The most economical new car you can afford, with the right features for your needs

b. The cheapest car you can find, period

c. The cheapest third-hand Mercedes/BMW/4WD that you can get your hands on, even if it's 20 years old and will cost you a fortune in petrol bills and maintenance.

5. **When you are caught in a traffic jam, you:**

a. Sit quietly in your lane listening to the radio - because maintaining discipline is in everyone's interest and will get everyone home faster

b. Sit fretting and fuming in your lane, cursing everyone around you and the idiots who cause these jams

c. Drive on to the pavement on the oncoming lane to try and gain a few metres on everyone else - because you must look after yourself

6. **The most meaningful expenditures in your life are:**

a. Your children's health and education

b. A big house with a swimming pool and a Range Rover

c. Beer and *nyama choma* every night

7. **The Meteorological Department has predicted torrential rains in coming months, you:**

a. Repair the hole in your roof immediately and have all the structures in your compound checked

b. Ask around to see what your neighbours are doing about it

c. Have another beer - those weathermen are all fools anyway

8. **Which group of Kenyans do you most admire?**

a. Rural women who bear the burden of work in this country and who struggle against the odds to make ends meet.

b. Learned Kenyans who have a long list of degrees from high-quality institutions.

   c.   Smart urban operators who make the right connections and who become millionaires overnight, as seen on TV's most gripping reality show, the Goldenberg Enquiry

9. **You run a small business, and you set your prices:**

   a.   At a level that meets your costs, provides you with an adequate profit margin, and offers good value to your customers

   b.   High enough to give you a good starting point from which to commence lengthy and noisy negotiations with all your customers

   c.   Higher than the prices charged by exclusive shops in London, with a readiness to go out of business (repeatedly) rather than bring prices down

10. **You go to a government office to obtain a simple license and find a long queue, so you:**

   a.   Find out whether this is indeed the right queue for you, ask a supervisor politely why this state of affairs exists, and write to the head of department and The *Nation's* "Watchman" column about it

   b.   Go away and come back another day

   c.   Join the queue and stand there for three hours in a stupor, and then come back the next day to do the same when you're told the forms aren't ready

11. **Who do you think should be responsible for your well-being?**

   a.   You alone.

b. The government.

c. Your employer and rich people of all types.

12. Who do you think is responsible for all the problems in your life?

a. You alone.

b. The government.

c. The colonialists, the IMF and World Bank, and multinational corporations.

13. You are watching a football tournament and a power blackout occurs, so you:

a. Switch on the kerosene lamp and start doing something else

b. Call KPLC's emergency hotline around 30 times until you finally go to sleep in the dark, exhausted

c. Gather a mob, go out into the streets and stone every single vehicle and pedestrian you see because they are, after all, responsible.

14. You are offered an opportunity to make a tidy sum of money illegally, so you:

a. Turn it down and consider reporting the offer to the authorities

b. Spend many sleepless nights wondering whether you should take the opportunity or not, and whether you'll get caught or not

c. Say hallelujah and grab it immediately! After all, you've spent your whole life waiting for exactly this kind of chance, and if you don't take it, some other smart fellow will!

15. You are offered an opportunity to work overseas, so you:

a. Consider the opportunity against the fact that Kenya is your home where your family, friends and all things familiar are

b. Look carefully at the benefits and take the opportunity if it offers more money and career advancement, with a view to coming back home eventually

c. Get the hell out on the next flight! Kenya is a total rat-hole and is doomed! Only fools stay here.

Scoring
Award yourself:
1 point for every '**a**' answer
3 points for every '**b**' answer
5 points for every '**c**' answer

Tot up your total: _____ points

Evaluation
15 points:
Who do you think you're kidding? This is a private quiz, and

you don't have to share your answers with anyone. Do the quiz again, and this time mark your true answers!

16 - 35 points:
You are part of a dying breed of Kenyans who still believe in values and principles. You are likely to be lonely and will die young, of unhappiness.

36 - 60 points:
You represent the vast majority of Kenyans, and now can feel that you truly belong here!

60+ points:
Congratulations! You win, everybody else loses. You are a true modern Kenyan. When you next ask why this country is in such a mess, refer back to this quiz, and then go to the nearest mirror.

June 2004

What we say versus what we mean

Let's begin with our peculiar talking habits. Kenyans are busy developing their very own vocabulary - in English.

This is a country where many say, "Good Mornings" when they address more than one person (as though there is more than one morning being considered). Or cheerfully tell you they are "Very OK" (two words in conflict) when asked how they are. Or shout "Imagine!" when highlighting something that has already happened. Or begin every other sentence with "Me, I..."

"Kenglish" can be great fun!

In Kenya, corporate people speak a language that sounds very important but means sweet nothing; for example, "Our mission is to leverage multiple platforms." The NGO world, not to be outdone, has developed its own dialect of meaningless drivel; for example, "A collaborative institutional framework between state and non-state actors." Politicians talk to voters as though they are addressing mentally ill ten-year-olds; for example, "There is no corruption in Kenya." Our diplomats maintain an utterly fake dialogue with "development partners", littered with noble-sounding but vapid phrases; for example, "We are continuing a partnership between our countries based on mutual respect to end global poverty."

Both sides realise this, but neither objects. Kenyans in posh jobs talk posh, but break out in Sheng the minute the boss isn't listening. The disease of inauthenticity has infected everyone.

You will find in the articles that follow the strangeness of Kenyan vocabulary. You will encounter words that don't mean what they mean to the rest of the world. You will recognise phrases that we routinely misuse. I hope they provoke you into saying what you mean.

A beginner's guide
to Kenyan vocabulary

Much confusion is caused in this country by the fact that many words mean something other than their common meaning. A great number of people out there have an enduring interest in the affairs and enterprises of this land: from investors to development partners; students to learned professors; tourists to journalists. All of these people face this daunting prospect: as soon as they pass through Immigration Control, certain English words cease to mean what they used to. So, as a public service to all our foreign friends, I thought I should offer a quick guide to Kenyan vocabulary.

Road lanes

The first item to grapple with is what you see on the roads. There are no road lanes in Kenya; those yellow lines you see on the roads exist merely to provide a pastime for large gangs of painters, and as a means of official support for our paint companies. Road lanes in Kenya do not demarcate anything at all. You are permitted to drive in (or on) any lane you wish. You may do this while shouting on two mobile phones, flicking FM radio channels, beating a small child and simultaneously sipping a Sprite. You may also change your mind as to your preferred lane at any time, without the need to warn others. Indeed you will soon realise that unless you know how to weave in and out of lanes at a high speed, you could spend your remaining days stuck behind a huge truck belching toxic smoke into your lungs in the "fast" lane.

Rush hour

Still on the subject of our world-famous roads, "rush hour" refers to the time of day when gangs of painters rush to our busiest highways to paint the road lanes (see above). It is traditional that this activity can only be conducted when there are the most vehicles on a road, for maximum impact. So, when you find yourself seething in a hot car at five o'clock on a Friday, rest assured that you will eventually discover twenty or so painters painting a single line (crookedly) having blocked all lanes bar one. Try not to be in a hurry; it doesn't help anyone.

Idler

You could be forgiven for imagining that this word refers to the armies of unemployed you see on the streets and public parks whose only known pastime is to await a mugging so that a quick lynching of the mugger can liven up an otherwise dreary day. But idlers are not just the unemployed in Kenya. We have plenty of idlers in seemingly gainful employment, particularly in high public office. Many view their duties with idle curiosity and professional disdain, and have no intention of ever breaking a sweat in the name of responsibility. MPs, mayors and assorted mandarins tend to inhabit the professional idler class. Look out for them.

Investor

Some of you may describe yourselves using this common word, meaning that you are someone who places money into ventures with a view to making a profit. In Kenya, however, you will find yourself in unseemly company. We attract the world's detritus here. As an "investor" you may find yourself rubbing shoulders with: ghostly figures hiding behind phantom companies creating scandals that never were; Mafiosi types trying to recreate microcosms of their own lands here, with sunshine attached; landowners who own fifty-thousand-acre farms that their grandfathers bought for a few beads, and who want to be allowed to shoot animals in sport to sustain their properties; and people who shout "investment!" when they buy a chair (second-hand) for their office. All of these investors like to think that the country is carried on their shoulders, and that they should receive tax breaks and ethics holidays. Be prepared to lobby loudly alongside them.

Aware

This is an odd word in Kenya, for it means the opposite of its dictionary definition. "I am not aware" is the most common expression, by far, used by public officials; yet it means this: "I know damn well what you're talking about, and yes, I did it and you know I did it and I know I did it and my children know I did it, but I will maintain a glazed expression in the face of all questioning, until the questions go away." So be aware of "aware".

Leadership

Here's an interesting one. You might imagine that a leader is one who sets an example, shows the way, takes the initiative, or does many other good things. Nope. Not in Kenya. A leader, quite simply, is anyone who has a large expensive car. There is no other qualification required. Without a swank Mercedes or a plush 4X4, you cannot lead. So if you already have one of these vehicles, lead on *Bwana*! We will all follow in your tread marks.

Famine

This word has a particular technical meaning in Kenya. It refers to an annual event whereby millions go hungry and thousands die for the cameras. This event is famous worldwide, and attracts swarms of onlookers: media types, rock stars, economists, aid workers, politicians, corporate donors with large dummy cheques, and rich housewives carrying a few bags of flour they have bought from their social-club kitty. Lately, the event has also started to attract the attention of dog-food makers. The famine is the time of year we all feel good about ourselves and demonstrate our community spirit. Except those dying, of course. But they're OK, they know it's all for a good cause. Book early.

Resign

A word that you will be hard put to find in Kenya. No one resigns from high office. People are sacked, fired, dropped, transferred, reshuffled and redeployed. They are shown the door and escorted to the gate. Once in a while, somebody will be forced to quit under pressure, or will go to pre-empt a sacking, usually after much elbowing by donors. A few may quit in a huff after being sidelined. Others might make a dramatic departure to create a political crisis. But resign on principle? Resign to take responsibility? Step aside to allow investigations to take place? Not really. Psychologists will tell you that most ministers demonstrate the symptoms of obsessive love for their cars and offices. Most have to be dragged from their desks kicking and screaming. Crowbars and strong solvents are needed to separate their beloved seats from their posteriors.

Hope

And finally, a word that means what you think it does. And how! For whatever happens here, we don't lose hope. We are amongst the poorest nations on earth, but we aim for the stars. Everything can be in disarray, but we will not forget to smile and look forward. This is one of the defining features of Kenyans: we believe things will get better. We may be led by those who denude us, but that's no reason to feel down. Amidst all the carjackings and collapsing buildings, we see a better future. This belief is what sustains us. And when a leadership emerges that can channel this unique energy, we will make the leap into sustained prosperity. We will. In the Kenyan breast, hope does spring eternal.

February 2006

The lies we tell - every day

Language is important. Words matter. It was with these sentiments in mind that I began noticing how many of us say things that we just don't mean. I'm not referring to the glib things we say that are economical with the truth; I'm more concerned about those expressions we routinely deploy that actually mean the EXACT OPPOSITE of what we really think. We all use them, every day. Don't believe me? Read on.

"With all due respect"
Come on, admit it: you used this one just yesterday. Admit also that what you really meant was "with the greatest contempt." This phrase is deployed when we think the person we're addressing is an imbecile, but who might well take violent umbrage if this is pointed out. So, we offer our "respect" to preface a derisive put-down.

"This will be a short speech"
If you hear this one and they haven't locked the doors yet, depart in haste. No one has ever launched his or speech with the truth, which is: "This will be an endless, humourless and pointless treatise on every single thing that has ever concerned me. Prepare to have the life-force bored out of You." Members of the captive audience should come prepared - with a discreet iPod, for example, or knowledge of Zen meditation. Otherwise prepare for a near-death experience; this phrase signals great danger.

"Listen, my friend"
"Friend" here is used in the loosest possible way; loose enough, in fact, to mean "enemy". We don't need to call our true friends "friends" at all. We only do that when the person in question is

anything but a friend. And it usually leads to a terribly unfriendly remark. When politicians hear themselves being referred to as friends by other politicos, their ears prick up. They know trouble is coming.

"Just between you and me"

Rest assured, this leads to something the whole world either knows or is about to find out. "A secret is something you tell one other person", that great lyricist Bono once wrote (before he became a foreign-aid fanatic). And he was right. The urge to spill beans and let cats out of bags is universal. So is the need to pretend that we value discretion and confidentiality.

"In all honesty"

What does that even mean? Is there something other than "all honesty"? Warning: untruth coming! Someone is about to feed you a falsehood, but wants to cloak himself in virtue while doing it. Whatever you are told after that opening you should consume with much salt.

"I'm not aware"

Ah, the politicians' favourite in Kenya. This one has the unique feature of being simultaneously true and untrue. True, because politicians are demonstrably not aware of anything that is really important to the people. Untrue because leaders and bureaucrats invariably use this phrase when they know exactly what happened, who stole the money, and where the bodies are hidden. I suggest a change to the laws of the land for courts to recognise "I'm not aware" as a clear admission of guilt.

"I don't like gossip, but..."

We all know what this one means: I love gossip! I love it when someone fills me in on the latest juicy office affair. It makes my day when you tell me about who is suspected to have stolen money at her last job. I want to do cartwheels when I hear the latest misfortunes to befall the people I despise. And rejoice, I'm about to tell you everything!

"I'm no fool"

This one was best said by the playwright Wilson Mizner: "A fellow who's always declaring he's no fool usually has his suspicions." Don't use this one. Even those who haven't questioned your intelligence yet will begin to wonder. People who aren't fools don't need to say so.

"We have delivered commendable returns to shareholders in a difficult environment by focusing operations on enterprise-wide customer-centric realignment."

This sort of garbage is often found in the CEO's statement of annual reports of the more desperate corporations. Translation: "We're in deep trouble. We don't have a clue what to do next. We're going to fire a lot of people anyway. We'll blame it on external factors, and hide our ineptitude behind bizarre jargon that no one understands." Recommendation to shareholders: sell.

"Thank you for calling; how may I help you?"

Found on the training script of every customer-service line and call centre. Sadly, anyone who has actually observed these people at work knows what they're really thinking: "Damn it! Another caller. Did you have to call now, you twit? Is there nothing you are able to solve by yourself? Go on, bore me with your complaints and your whining. I'm not listening anyway, and I'll only refer you to someone else. Where's that doughnut?"

That's it, folks. Delighted to have had your company today - have a nice day!

May 2007

The stock phrases
we love misusing

One thing we seem to sorely lack in this country is linguistic intelligence. We are acutely unaware of the power of words, and how to harness and use that power. As a result, we use the same old clichéd phrases every day. These phrases are so overused that they actually cease to have meaning. We hear them. We ignore them. We carry on as before.

The writer George Orwell wrote: "[Language] becomes ugly and inaccurate because our thoughts are foolish, but the slovenliness of our language makes it easier for us to have foolish thoughts." Most of our thoughts are indeed foolish, but by using so many pat, meaningless, banal phrases all the time, we are reinforcing the foolishness of our thoughts.

So here is a guide to Kenyan phraseology, to help you understand what foolish thoughts are behind the phrases that have become our common currency.

"Carry your own cross"
If you spend any amount of time listening to Kenyan politicians (why you would want to do that I don't know but, hey, it's a free world) there is one phrase you can be sure of hearing every single day: "Let everyone carry their own cross." I imagine it evokes images of the suffering of Jesus when He was so unjustly crucified by a cruel world. Politicians like this symbolism: it paints them as long-suffering champions of the poor. If only.

What "carry your own cross" also conveys is that there are many, many crosses to be carried, and no one can help anyone else carry theirs. As the phrase is most often used in the context of corruption, I can only agree with this reading: the crosses of graft and plunder abound. The strange thing is that no leader or man of means has ever carried one! Not one, in 45 years of self-realisation as a nation. Crosses are carried by the poor and by the honest in Kenya, not by the leeches that live off them. I can only hope that retribution of biblical proportions awaits those who keep mouthing this phrase.

"When/Where did the rain start beating us?"

This has become a favourite of the media, especially since we began our downward spiral in early 2008. Now it is a question asked all the time, and a very silly one too. If you Google it, your top results will all be Kenyan! The question presupposes that our woes fall from heaven, that they are the result of forces external to us, and that we are the innocent victims of powerful but undeserved punishment.

What nonsense.

The rain that is beating us is caused by each and every one of us. Heaven or Hell have nothing to do with it. The rain beats us because we deserve to be beaten, to be cleansed, be deluged. We are a society that is in severe moral deficit. We don't care about higher purpose, we don't give a damn about our fellow humans, we steal and grab and cheat at every turn. We deserve the battering of the rain, and more. Ironically, if we carry on cutting down trees at the rate we are, we won't have to worry about this question at all very soon...

"The customer is king"

The business world is not immune to banality. Every business you encounter in Kenya will chant a variant of this phrase, in unison. Not one will mean it. There should be a law in Kenya preventing companies from using these words, for they are in danger of believing they live up to it. As i have written in my book, *Crown Your Customer*, the customer is no king in Kenya; he is a serf, a pauper, a vagabond.

If the customer were king, why would he be met with unsmiling, unschooled and unhinged customer assistants everywhere? Why would he be abused and ignored on a daily basis? Why would he complain until kingdom come without ever being taken seriously? Why would he encounter defective products and dismal service everywhere? Is that not what happens to you?

"The global economic meltdown has created challenging conditions"
Let me end with another example of how we want to believe our troubles are visited on us from elsewhere. The world is in financial turmoil: excellent! This gives everyone from the government to leading companies an excuse on which to pin their own under-performance. It's not us, it's the credit crunch. Every government statement, every company financial report will make reference to this in 2009.

As though our economy was not going to spiral downwards anyway! Did we not do enough with our own hands to wreck our livelihoods and resources at the beginning of 2008? Do we need a reason from outside? Is the outright concerted looting of public coffers that we see every day not enough to finish us? Are our companies making any effort to become world-class in the first place, that the world's troubles should affect them?

Until we learn honesty in our discourse, we will keep spouting this foolishness.

March 2009

CHAPTER TWO
Making money, Kenya-style

Let's admit it. What is the one thing ALL Kenyans love? It's not their mothers. It is money. In Kenya, you can never have enough money. There are Kenyans who are as rich as virtually anyone in the world, even though they live in one of the world's poorest nations. There are people here who are sitting on piles of cash that would sustain perhaps five future generations in princely style.

But those are just a chosen few. Most Kenyans don't possess more money than the change in their pockets on a given day. It is a country of awful contrasts, where some live like royals and most live like rats. In a modern democracy, this is puzzling: why don't more Kenyans feel resentment at seeing the bloated rich in their midst? Why are we still organised like a medieval feudal state when it comes to inequality?

Because everyone admires the rich, that's why. If there's anything everyone from the matatu tout to the clerical officer dreams of being, it's rich. Not just rich enough to be free, mind you, but obscenely, grotesquely rich. That is why we adore the politicians who can show us their motorcades of swanky limos and their collection of palatial homes. That is why we detest the politicians who are too poor to give handouts, and never vote for them.

In most countries, politicians are at pains to hide their wealth. In India, they wear simple white clothing. In Europe, they go around on bicycles. Not so in Kenya. Here, politicians want to pretend they have more than they're showing you. Many a retired politician goes to great lengths to demonstrate how being out of office has not affected his bank balance, and will want to point out all the properties and farms he owns. This is because voters prefer the rich, hoping they will get a share of the wealth somehow. Kenyans are known across the region as being money-mad.

Once in while, I would forget my anger over this state of affairs and try to smile about it. This resulted in the two pieces that follow, giving free advice about how to make money in Kenya...

The Chapter ends with another "Kenyanness" quiz.

The top ways to make money in Kenya

There must be thousands of you dreaming of joining Kenya's Rich List someday. So I thought I should offer young people a guide to making it big in Kenya. If making money is your thing, then here are the Top Four ways of doing it. For all you youngsters out there with dollar signs in your eyes, here is some serious career advice, the type you won't get in your university careers office. The list is presented in reverse order of money-making potential.

(4) Start a monopoly company

Monopolies are great. The customer has no choice but to buy from you, and you can make the quality of your product or service as shoddy as you like. Cut costs to the bone, don't invest in customer service, set your margins to be as healthy as you like. It's a license to print money. But how do you get into the game? Well, you must be willing to invest some capital in befriending the right officials, and obtaining a license giving you the exclusive right to conduct a particular activity, preferably for five years or more.

Once these bureaucrats are on your side, they will issue helpful statements to the public explaining the need for stability in the market, the desirability of nurturing local entrepreneurs, etc. Of course, in exchange they will expect to partake in the profit margin, so set it high enough! Once these conditions are in place, you can happily fleece the public for years, as well as retard all progress in the market. Outdoor advertising, airport services, mining, telecommunications, and power generation are all good potential monopolies to consider.

(3) Open a bank

Another great Kenyan money-spinner! Here, you have two options: you can either open a dodgy bank for crooks like yourself, or open a serious bank for the respectable public. In the former option, you need to have a network of shady characters with money to hide. These people will provide you with your first deposits and give you an asset base. You will then open up your doors to the general public (also known as the mugs) and offer amazingly high interest rates.

You can't lose money appealing to people's greed. You will be surprised how many of these people will come rushing in to support your bank! After building your deposit base, you can give hundreds of millions out in loans to yourself, to companies in which you have an interest, to friends and relatives, etc. These loans need never be repaid. Eventually, of course, the whole bank will collapse. By then, you will have used the "loans" to set yourself up for life.

The second banking option is to open a mainstream, respectable bank that does not engage in any funny business. The results here may not be instantaneous, but they are eye-popping nonetheless. Your target market is the teeming multitudes that have had their fingers burned by investing in dodgy banks (described above). These poor souls (also known as suckers) will have been so frightened by the experience of losing all their money that they will now value integrity above all else in a bank. They will be ripe for further denuding.

Once you have invested in your reputation, you can offer these customers ridiculously high interest rates on their deposits, and they will not even squeal. You can charge them for literally everything they do in your bank, including stepping in through the door, walking on your carpet, and breathing the air you helpfully provide. You can be rude to them and mess up their records for years, without ever hearing a whimper. In this model, you will give out loans on generally sound projects, and charge handsomely. The spread you make on these loans will go straight to shareholders, your costs having been covered by all the charges above. So go for banking, youngsters – it's pure gravy.

(2) Position yourself in or around a parastatal

Parastatals are superb money-making vehicles. They are usually monopolies (see (4) above) and do not have unhelpful competitors making life difficult. They are state-owned, therefore customers' expectations are usually very low. This means that you will be spared unnecessary concern about customer care or product quality. The shareholder is the government, which means you don't have to worry about making a profit. You can lose money for years, preferably to yourself. If you find a career in parastatals interesting, focus on the key function known as procurement. This is where 90 per cent of the activity takes place – parastatals do little else other than purchase cars, equipment, cranes etc, at spectacular prices.

Of course, you can also be on the other side, and supply things to a parastatal. Some of Kenya's most notable fortunes have been made in this way. The only investment you will need to make is in entertaining the parastatal's key officers. Your company does not have to actually manufacture, supply or provide any goods or services – don't let that worry you for a moment. You will be paid money for thin air. What's the margin on that? Exciting, eh?

(1) Become a politician

By far the quickest and most dramatic method of making money in Kenya is to join politics. Here, you will need some initial investment to give the appearance of being rich in the first place – Kenyans don't vote for poor people. So you must have a flashy car and a large rural house. Take out loans for these (preferably from a dodgy bank – see (3) above), and don't worry: you will repay them, if at all you have to, in a year or two.

A politician's life, if you play your cards right, is one long gravy train. If you control a good, solid tribal voting bloc, you will find yourself being allocated vast tracts of land, at zero cost, by the government of the day. You will be given shareholdings in major corporations and asked to join their boards of directors, again for no outlay. You will find that most things in life become free: hotel stays for your family, first-class travel, major purchases, etc. For some reason, people will stop charging you for things. This is the big one, youngsters: develop a loud voice, frighten your tribe into thinking it needs you in order to survive – and go for it!

So, young Kenyans, these are the top ways to make the big money. Do it right, and you may make enough for your next five generations. There will be costs, of course: you will stop sleeping well at night; you will worry incessantly about losing your money; you will never love or trust another human being again; you will almost certainly spend some time in jail. But these are minor matters, surely, and unlikely to deter someone of your calibre.

The alternative is to work hard, develop real skills, and lead a clean life. Unlike the four methods outlined above, this route has no guarantee of success whatsoever, and may take years and years to come to fruition. Who wants that?

December 2003

A guide to the best professions in Kenya

We are a nation of creative entrepreneurs, we tell ourselves. Our ability to get something from nothing, to create hot air from thin air is the stuff of legends, we tell visitors. A Working Nation, half a million jobs a year? Ha, we tell our leaders: we have no need for the platitudes that feed the multitudes. We know exactly how to make money, and here's the beauty of it all – we don't even have to work to make it!

For the few of you out there who still haven't found Rich Plaza on Lazy Lane, here's a quick guide to the best occupations in Kenya. Easy money awaits!

Elder for hire
This is one of the top ways to earn a crust while doing nothing. Simply advertise your services as the most respected community elder ready to bequeath 'sole leader' or 'tribal spokesman' status on gullible politicians. Believe me, there will be a long line of wannabe presidents lining up to buy your services. But there are a few niceties to observe if you want to make it in this lucrative field.

First, you must actually look like an elder, so matted grey hair, a long beard and scanty attire are a must. If you don't look the part, fret not: modern makeup can do wonders. Second, you need to learn some interesting chants and carry some strong-smelling potions, not to mention a range of unusual headgear. Again, no capital necessary: nature will provide all the reeds, feathers, skins and pastes you are likely to need. Lastly, you would be

39

wise not to confine yourself to one tribe: learn the rites of all of them and widen your market. So stop disappointing, and start anointing!

Politician's flunkey

This is a big growth area. Politicians of all parties require a vast entourage of aides, hangers-on and bodyguards these days. The more the merrier, as it projects an image of power and popularity. Most are willing to pay decent money for long-term flunkeys. Your only duties will be to sit under a tree until the Big Man emerges, run like mad to open his car door, jump into your designated chase car, and then sit pretty with your nose out of the window as your convoy ploughs through Nairobi at high speed. Once you arrive at your destination, find another tree to sit under. Occasionally, you may have to attack journalists and break their cameras, but most of the time the job just entails looking seriously daunting.

Tools of the trade? Just a dark suit and dark shades. Education is actually an impediment; dump it if you have it.

Government of Kenya employee

Another good one, so target any ministry, department or parastatal that offers itself. Your best bet is to study the names and origins of those in charge, and find one whose leader comes from within a 100 km radius of your home village. This will allow you to use your trump cards - tribe, clan and kinship - to land the job. Shouldn't be difficult.

Be careful, though: there are two types of GoK employees. The first, a very small, very hardworking group, does all the work of government and carries the nation on its shoulders; the second, the vast majority, does absolutely nothing. Make sure you don't end up in the first group by mistake. Once ensconced in the second group, you can look forward to a life of idle pleasure and many side businesses. At some stage, however, the World Bank will appear and demand that you and many thousands like you must be retrenched as you are a drain on the economy. Don't worry; this process will take at least 10 years to effect. And when it does happen, you will receive a handsome payoff that will give you a life of idle pleasure and many side businesses. Enjoy!

Professional dependant

It doesn't get better than this. You need never work again, yet you will have all your needs taken care of by a close relative. Join the multitudes of Kenyans who have found out that once "one of your own" makes it big, dozens of relatives can live off the takings. All you need to perfect are your hard luck stories: the paralysed cuticle that prevents you from working; the collapsed bank that took all your savings; the thirty-five younger siblings to school, feed and clothe.

Keep reminding the successful relative of the happy days you spent together as children in the village; the time you gave him your last maize cob when he had nothing; what his mother said to you before she died; and how your sister is his wife and your niece is his mistress. Usually works a treat.

Rap artist

If fame is your thing, then this is the one for you. First, shed some clothes (particularly underwear). Then, get yourself a snappy moniker like L'il Zit or Shameless or even just '?'. Next, sit down and write some words, any words, at random: Your opening line could be "whack smack street smart glue train", for example. Now replace every fourth word with an obscenity. Lastly, go to Luthuli Avenue and find one of those back-street geeks who own a computer and a synthesiser. He will add a snazzy tune to your lyrics. You are ready for the big time.

If you play your cards right, an adoring public will sing your songs and worship you like a living god. Respect!

Mamluki

Lastly, the big one. If you really want to do nothing and be paid well for it in Africa, a mercenary's life is the one for you. Some of you may be getting worried here: do I have to pack a gun and dodge bullets in far-off deserts? Nah, you're thinking seventies. A modern operator drives different cars every day, wears sunglasses even when alone in a dark room at midnight, and wears 'bling-bling' that's measured in kilos, not carats.

Expensive, you say? Don't worry, you won't have to part with a penny. In any case, gold-plating is an excellent thing. The only work you may have to do is to look ridiculous and play with dogs. In return, you will rub shoulders with the high and mighty and the low and flighty. The bold and the beautiful will be your companions, and the days of your life will be spent in 7th heaven.

What skills do you need? Ah, OK, this one's a bit tricky. You may need many passports, for one thing. You will need to travel through Dubai regularly, even though your citizenship will be denied by all known governments. You will require many mysterious backers who will stay in the shadows and get you to front their deals. But the real clincher: to be a modern-day mercenary in modern-day Africa, you must be light-skinned. Any skin shades darker than beige need not apply. You just won't have the credibility, you see.

April 2006

How Kenyan Are You?
(Part 2)

Lets end this chapter with another quick quiz,. As we were grappling with our "mamluki" visitors in 2006, we were also all proclaiming our patriotism with new car stickers. I decided to put all this newfound nationalistic sentiment to the test...

Patriotism is back on the agenda. We are at that stage in our evolution where we need to define what a 'Kenyan' is. Nations only prosper when its people possess common cause and unity of purpose. But what, exactly, is a Kenyan? Is it something defined by your passport or ID card? Your domicile? By what you say, or by what beats deep inside your heart? Is it about bravado or about behaviour?

This is not an easy thing to assess. There are Kenyans of all colours and shapes. They live right here, and also across the globe. What do they share in common? I think it's time we all assessed ourselves, so I attach another quick test of what it means to be Kenyan. Enjoy!

1. **You express your patriotism by:**

   a. Working hard for myself and for the people around me, by contributing my knowledge and skills, and by standing up for what is right in the country.

   b. Minding my own affairs, paying my taxes and living within the law.

   c. Stealing anything I can lay my hands on whilst displaying a patriotic car sticker.

2. **You consider a safe driving speed as:**

    a. The speed limit set by the law.

    b. A reasonable velocity at which I can control my vehicle and respond to the unexpected.

    c. 150 kph (urban); 250 kph (extra-urban).

3. **You are driving a car at high speed while eating a banana. What do you do with the banana skin?**

    a. Keep it in the car until I get home, so that I can dispose of it properly.

    b. Toss it out of the window.

    c. Try to throw it into someone else's car.

4. **If you had all the money you needed, what would you eat?**

    a. My diet is already balanced and nutritious; with more money I would only buy better-quality ingredients.

    b. *Nyama Choma*, for breakfast, lunch and dinner.

    c. I'd stop eating all these 'native' foods, and be able to afford burgers and fried chicken every day.

5. **If you got a good job overseas, to leave the country, it would take you:**

    a. As long as necessary to consult all the appropriate people and come to a considered decision on such a weighty matter.

    b. As long as it takes to wind up my affairs here.

    c.   How long does it take to get to the airport? So long, suckers!

6. **Kenya's national greeting is:**

    a.   Jambo.

    b.   Sema.

    c.   Wassup, dawg?

7. **The centre of gravity of your world is:**

    a.   My home town or village.

    b.   Nairobi.

    c.   Boston, USA.

8. **The living figure most worthy of Kenyans' admiration is:**

    a.   Nelson Mandela.

    b.   Barack Obama.

    c.   50 Cent.

9. **Who is responsible for your well-being?**

    a.   I am.

    b.   The Government of Kenya.

    c.   Bill Gates. (Do you have his mobile number, so that I can flash him?).

10. How many members of your extended family still live in Kenya?

a. All of them.

b. About half of them.

c. I'm the last one left (and I'm packing).

11. The universal formula for success in business is:

a. Understand your customers, look after your staff and deliver value to your shareholders - better than anyone else does.

b. Mind the cents and the dollars will look after themselves.

c. Squeeze every last drop out of your customers, frisk your thieving staff and lock them in every day, cheat on your taxes and don't have shareholders other than yourself.

12. Translate the first two lines of your national anthem into English:

a. "O God of all creation, bless this our land and nation."

b. "O God of my fixation, bless me and my relations."

c. "Yo Gawd, gimme salvation, get me some of that dollar remuneration."

Scoring

Award yourself:

1 point for every '**a**' answer,
3 points for every '**b**' answer
5 points for every '**c**' answer

Tot up your total: _____ points.

Evaluation

12 - 23 points

You seem to understand that there is more to patriotism than slogans and stickers, that it is about what you feel for your compatriots and what you are willing to do for others. But you are the ghost of the Kenyan past, and the waning hope for the Kenyan future. You are part of an endangered species - there are probably no more than a dozen of you left in the wild. Please stand for president before you're wiped out.

24 - 49 points

You are a very typical Kenyan. You mind your own business, live in your narrow little world, keep your head down, and never protest. Everything is someone else's fault, and this country is always going to the dogs. You will never personally do anything about it. So keep waiting for the saviour to arrive, and have some more goat ribs while you're at it.

50+ points

You must have done this quiz online - or have you not got your Green Card yet? Keep trying, dude - plenty of *jamaaz* making a pile Stateside. We used to sell tea and flowers abroad; now you are our biggest export. Long may you reign in far-off lands (the farther the better).

August 2006

CHAPTER THREE
Oh, our politicians...

If there was a prize for the world's worst politicians, our boys (and some girls) would win it hands down. Rarely has there been a place or time in history when leaders have been so detached from their followers, and so unconcerned about the general good.

Our politicians are famously thick-skinned, though: no amount of criticism, no matter how justified, will make them feel any regret or shame. The bizarre thing is Kenyans' willingness to stay engrossed in the circus of politics, following every new alliance and party with great interest, even though nothing changes. The musical chairs game at the top continues apace, with Kenyans clapping to the tune and paying the bill at the end.

Kenyans are famously and peculiarly obsessed with politics. The daily headlines of our newspapers and radio and TV news shows are all political. Newspapers sell more on days when a big political story is raging. In bars and tearooms across the land, the talk is all about which politician is doing what. Listen in on the conversations of our ubiquitous watchmen, as I often do: they will invariably be discussing who will win the next election, even if it's four years away.

Every so often, I abandon the withering critique and the righteous tone in favour of sarcasm. It may be the lowest form of wit, but it suits a place where the lowest form of life often rises to the top. In the first of the five pieces that follow, I offer advice on how to become a Kenyan politician. For the next two, I invented the character of Dr Abunwasi bin Uwongo. This was when Kenya came up with the position of Government Spokesman, and managing the story seemed to become more important than telling the truth. So I thought up my own parallel spin doctor, complete with impressive acronym and educational credentials from my own university - well, almost!

The next two pieces take aim at Kenya's parliamentarians, as unruly a crew of ruffians as you are likely to encounter in any dark alley in the world. And paid world-class salaries to boot...

If you want to join the ranks of our leaders, take the leadership quiz that follows.

This section ends with a solution to the problem of woeful leadership: Men, let's face the fact that we've screwed up big time and hand over power to women...

How to succeed
as a politician in Kenya

If you are young and ambitious, the biggest career in Kenya is to become a politician. So pay attention, youngsters – you could make more money and command more power than you can dream of.

The wonderful thing about becoming a successful politician in Kenya is that, unlike other ventures, you require little start-up capital. Many of our leading lights have emerged from the grimiest ghettos and the remotest rural wastelands. Today, they own vast (and undeclared) tracts of land, ride around in chauffeured limousines and have dozens of sycophants at their beck and call. You too can have all this. To start, all you need is a certain type of personality.

Do you have a violent, overwhelming desire to control others? Did you always rule over your siblings (including the older ones)? Were your parents always a little scared of you? Do you fly into uncontrollable rages when you can't have your own way? Do you believe, with absolute and unassailable certainty, that you are always right? If you answered an emphatic 'yes' to most of these questions – perfect! You are top politician material. You will go very far indeed.

Still on personality: do you want it all? Do you find yourself salivating in public as you daydream about huge four-wheel drive vehicles with curtained windows? Do you believe a successful Kenyan should own at least five houses? Will you stop at nothing to achieve these goals? Do your intestines twist painfully when you see people who already have these things? Again, if you answered 'yes', you're made of the right stuff.

If you passed the personality test, you're already on your way. All you need is a strategy. Fortunately, this is not difficult. Just follow a few straightforward steps, and the kingdom of wealth, power and glory is yours.

First and foremost: focus on tribe. Tribe is the defining political unit in Kenya. To succeed in politics, you must control your tribal vote. Hopefully, you belong to one of the larger tribal groupings. If not, never fret – even smaller tribes are always needed in political equations. The key thing to remember is that you must stop your tribesmen from thinking of themselves as Kenyans. Any tendencies towards national unity must be stamped out immediately. The reason is simple: you will lose control of your votes if people start identifying with others. You will lose the emotional pull of tribal sentiment. Heaven forbid, you may even have to start campaigning on issues! No politician wants this. It is far, far easier to win votes on ethnicity.

The key, however, is fear. You must make sure that your tribe is scared stiff of all other tribes. You must instil the fear of irrelevance and even of annihilation in your brethren. You must constantly make dark references to the ethnic clashes of the past, and convince your people of the vast conspiracy that is assembled against them. If your tribe has already provided a president, you must talk of how the presidency naturally belongs to your group. If it has not, you must agitate that it is now the turn of your people to 'eat'. Think tribe, and you'll go far.

Secondly, please remember: you go into politics for yourself. It is the most self-centred of careers. Yet you must never reveal this. You must always wear a pious expression that shows you carry the pain of the people in your bosom. You must avoid your naturally belligerent expression that probably frightens little children and dogs. When appearing at a commission of inquiry to explain your sins (as you very probably will at some stage in your career) you must avoid having the visage of a cattle rustler. Some professional training by media consultants would be a very worthwhile investment for you.

The third key factor: you must lose all sense of shame. If you are considering a career in politics, the chances are high that you will not be in possession of this emotion in the first place. But you must make sure that you remove all traces of this unnecessary feeling, for you will find it a great burden in years to come.

After all, you will have to do many, many shameful things as a politician. You will have to make friends, swear unshakeable loyalty to them, and then drop them like hot potatoes at a moment's notice. You will have to tell lies in public in the presence of cameras and microphones, and then claim you were misquoted. You will have to put your signature to many memoranda of understanding, and then deny their existence.

If you feel even an iota of shame when you do these excellent things, you will be hopelessly handicapped as a politician. It will cramp your style and reduce your effectiveness. The only sure way to rid yourself of this problem is to seek medical intervention. The mysterious doctors who inhabit the shadowy corridors of big-name hospitals offer a discreet operation – excision of the 'shame gland'. This little-known gland is located close to the prostate gland, and is easily removed. The operation is painful and expensive, and you will have to lie on your stomach for a week to recover – but it's well worth it. Many luminaries have had it done before you. It is rarely fatal.

The fourth critical success factor in politics: assemble the right sort of family. A good, wholesome and photogenic family is vital in Kenyan politics today. There are, however, some simple rules to follow. If you are a man, it is a good idea to have at least two wives. Of these, one should be young, lissom and glamorous. The other should be robust and matronly. It often helps if one is of foreign extraction– this confers a certain cosmopolitan status on you. European wives are preferred in this regard; Americans are to be avoided.

If you are a female political aspirant, having two husbands – in any sense whatsoever – would be an unmitigated disaster. A quiet, sensible, professional man who stays away from the limelight is preferred – a doctor or accountant would be perfect. If your husband is a bellicose drunkard or a scheming lawyer – dump him now. He will ruin your career one day.

So there you are, four simple rules to follow. Follow them well, and you will certainly go far. Of course, not all politicians are like this; some are gentle, well-meaning souls who join politics for the good of the common man and to develop the nation. By and large, they fail. The sure way to succeed is to dismiss all thoughts of doing any good. In fact, you and most of your colleagues will be the single biggest impediment to development in this country. Prepare to join a celebrated procession of politicians who have adorned this nation since independence.

April 2004

An exclusive interview with the new government spin-doctor

Following on from the appointment of the official Government Spokesman some months ago, the Government this week announced the formation of a new office – that of the Government Spin Doctor. Dr. Abunwasi bin Uwongo was appointed to this important new post yesterday, and he granted the *Sunday Nation* an exclusive first interview. He explains his role and his interpretation of recent events in this wide-ranging interview.

Q: Dr. Uwongo, lets start with the new post. We all refer to you as the Government Spin Doctor, but what is your official title?
A: I am the Secretary for Policy Interpretation of Government Actions (PIGA).

Q: Why does Kenya need such an office?
A: Well, it has become obvious that Kenyans simply do not understand what the government is up to these days. The official Government Spokesman is doing his best to explain, but he is saddled with two jobs: that of providing facts and official positions; and that of making generous interpretations of events. He is a decent fellow who has been taking unnecessary flak and is feeling rather exposed. So we decided to limit him to the basic job of giving facts and figures, whereas I will provide the spin and polish. Also, ministers are finding it increasingly difficult to tell barefaced lies without blushing and sweating, so I was called in to take this duty off them.

Q: And are you qualified for this post?

A: Certainly. I have a doctorate in the Comparative History of Fantasies and Fables from the London School of Truth Economics. I worked with a team that wrote Bill Clinton's speeches for many years. I have also worked with a number of leading advertising agencies in New York.

Q: And what persuaded you to return home? Was it the call of the soil? Or perhaps the need to contribute to the country's development?
A: No, I did it for the money.

Q: That's refreshingly honest. Will you retain the same candour for your government pronouncements?
A: Yes, you can trust me absolutely.

Q: Why is spin-doctoring necessary?
A: Well, we have worked out that Kenyans have no interest in the truth. It's too ugly. Even when the truth is quite blatantly and obviously apparent, they look away from it. They do not act on it. They are far more interested in story telling and fables. And I am just the man to spin tales.

Q: Let's move then to your position on this government's record so far. Kenyans are dissatisfied with all the broken promises on jobs, roads, power, etc. What do you say in the government's defence?
A: It's really very simple. Kenyans need to wise up. When this government said it would "create" half a million jobs, surely no one imagined it would do this itself? It was merely going to facilitate the creation of jobs by providing good government. In fact several million such jobs have been created – my department is preparing the figures. Equally, when we spoke of reforestation,

did you think ministers would plant trees? Of course not! Our job is to tell you how fast the forests are disappearing, so that you can organise yourselves to buy seedlings and plant trees. When there's a famine, our job is to provide photo opportunities for you to make donations. This is a modern government of enablers and facilitators.

Q: What about corruption?
A: What about it? Corruption is an inescapable fact of life. You are corrupt, and so, very certainly, am I. Let's face it – we are world leaders in corruption. Now that our athletics glory days are behind us, it's the only thing left that we're good at. Why not flaunt it? Ministers are merely showing the way. And Kenyans don't have any problem with corruption. When they hear of a scam, the only thing they lament is not being able to benefit from it themselves. We were only pretending to worry about corruption to appease the silly donors. So we have decided to stop faking it. We will soon open a university to teach graft and provide opportunities to all. We will even open an international consultancy office to bring in foreign exchange.

Q: But can you point to any achievements that this government has made?
A: Of course not. This is another example of Kenyans' naivety. Development is a process, not an event. We have provided some inputs to the process. The outputs are down to Kenyans. If nothing is happening, well, what are you people down there doing wrong? Take a hard look at yourselves!

Q: What exactly is it that government does, then?
A: Oh, a great deal. We prevent chaos in the country, for a start. All you tribal chauvinists would undoubtedly slaughter each

other with *pangas* if you didn't have ministers in large cars to look up to and admire. We give the appearance of order so that people remain civilised. Look around you: Somalia, Sudan, Rwanda – the difference is obvious!

Q: But people worry about insecurity...
A: There is no insecurity in this country. I've been here two days, and no one has attacked me. If you drive into forests to make phone calls, then you bring it upon yourself. If you stay in the right areas you'll be fine. Most violence results from domestic squabbles anyway.

Q: Does government do anything for the poor people of this country?
A: Of course! We give hope! It's called trickle-down economics. This is how it works: we give tax breaks and incentives at the EPZs. Investors looking for cheap labour and low taxes flock in to set up sweatshops. Your neighbour's son in Kakamega gets a job there. After some months, he visits home and comes to see you. He tells you stories about his grand life and gives your children some lollipops. They also aspire to go to Nairobi and buy their own lollipops. They become earners and spenders. That's trickle-down! It's what keeps the wheels of commerce rolling. It's all about aspirations.

Q: And will the poor one day become rich via trickle-down?
A: No, no, don't be ridiculous. There isn't enough money in Kenya for everyone to be rich! Isn't that obvious? Most of the poor have a duty to remain poor, otherwise there would be anarchy; only a few can get through at a time. And how would rich people feel rich if everyone had the same cars and houses as them? It's all about relativity and equilibria.

Q: Any final words?
A: Yes. Kenyans should not think running government is easy. Ministers are addressing complex and fluid situations every day. We are assembling structures and processes for the facilitation of economic development in a proactive and stakeholder-focused manner. All of this requires clear and persistent translation. Don't listen to journalists and NGO activists. They only agitate because they are not poor enough to be preoccupied by the search for food, and not rich enough to relax. I will be providing all the explanations you need in the months to come. I will be your guide all the way to voting day. It'll be fun!

September 2004

Whining Wafulas and Suspicious Swalehs: Dr Uwongo's new interview

The *Sunday Nation* dispatched a senior editor to the offices of the Government Spin Doctor: Dr. Abunwasi bin Uwongo, the Secretary for Policy Interpretation of Government Actions (PIGA). Dr. Uwongo, a graduate of the London School of Truth Economics, granted a rare exclusive interview to the *Sunday Nation*. A wide range of topics was covered, including this week's national budget. Excerpts:

Q: Dr. Uwongo, we have not seen much of you since your surprise appointment last year.
A: I have been overseas for much of the time, studying how they do spin-doctoring in the world's leading spin-countries: the USA, UK, Dubai, and the like. Those people are good. They have a lot to teach us. Even Botswana has employed some *mzungu* called McCall Smith or something like that to write a series of novels about the country. International bestsellers, every one of them! The tourists are pouring in! We must raise our game in Kenya. We're still designing posters with lions on them, and making TV adverts where a minister gives a speech. Out of date! Out of touch! Out of style! The message is everything. The package is the product. Spinning is winning. Illusion is expansion.

Q: Ah, so your trips are part of the millions spent by the government on overseas trips...
A: You know, I really have no idea why Kenyans have a problem with that. We must learn from the world! We must not reinvent the wheel every year! We must replicate, not isolate!

Q: Expensive mimicry, in other words?

A: Yes. No! Not mimicry – best practice! We must leave our drums behind, and embrace computers. We must kiss modern technology on the mouth!

Q: (Looks around.) Well, you have certainly done that here in your office. It is very large and lavishly equipped.

A: Yes, you have to give key people the democratic space in which to perform. If you confine people in hutches, you get rabbits. If you pay peanuts, you get monkeys. This government invests in the best.

Q: You seem to have taken over an entire floor. Was there not a free clinic here previously?

A: Yes, can you imagine? Queues of ugly people in rags with gaping wounds and sores! Blood everywhere! I soon put an end to that. The clinic has gone to Korogocho slums where it belongs, amongst the late-night revellers. We sanitised the whole floor and then my designers moved in. It's very tasteful now.

Q: Yes. Let's talk about this week's national budget. Your thoughts?

A: Growth, growth and more growth! Kenyans should prepare for take-off. 4.3 per cent today, 10 per cent tomorrow. We will be the new China.

Q: How so?

A: It's really very simple. Kenyans will now drink and smoke less. They will stop driving over roundabouts every Friday night, and stop coughing their way to early graves. Result: human capital gain! They will eat more ugali and drink more milk. Human capital gain! Girls will not miss school because they can't afford sanitary pads. Human capital gain! We are making investments in the working nation. The rest is down to Kenyans.

Q: But is the funding for all this largesse secure? Can we really reduce taxes and increase spending at the same time? Is the tax base that wide now, and our development partners so irrelevant? Is there not a danger of heavy borrowing to finance this budget, leading to a jump in interest rates?
A: Are you an economist? No. Am I? No. Is anyone in Kenya? Questionable. Let us not dabble in theories we don't even understand. Let us focus on the 'feel good' factor.

Q: Explain.
A: We have become a nation of Doubting Thomases, Whining Wafulas, Suspicious Swalehs and Chattering Cheges. We are aways complaining and pointing fingers. Is it any surprise we have stagnated for so long? For a nation to take off, it must feel good about itself. When people feel good, they work hard and pay taxes. They invest and spend. Feel-good is good-good.

Q: But what is there to feel good about for the 6 people out of every 10 who live below the poverty line?
A: That they are alive. That they are governed by visionary leaders. That they do not live in a country of bloody chaos, like their neighbours. That they have a million brothers and sisters in good jobs overseas sending them money every month. Really, there's so much to be grateful for, if only we think about it. It is you media people who keep focusing on the negative.

Q: But these "visionary leaders" appear to have a problem staying awake during the budget speech every year...
A: They are not sleeping. They are meditating. Do you understand

meditation? Focused attention. You Kenyan editors could do with some. The MPs are concentrating on the complexities of the budget.

Q: But they were snoring...
A: The best meditation techniques have some audial side effects.

Q: Let us turn to the state of the coalition. There appears to be some reduction in the squabbling of late.
A: There was never any squabbling. It was an invention by you editors to sell newspapers. The coalition has been in harmony since day one.

Q: But just last year we saw an MP attack a colleague at a public rally with a Fanta bottle. And another was reported to have said that his opponents would be "crushed like ants" if they visited his constituency.
A: More misreporting. I think you'll find that the first MP was offering his honourable colleague a soft drink. And the second actually said he would "brush the pants" of any visitors (he lives in a dusty constituency).

Q: Any final words?
A: Yes. Kenyans must stop pointing fingers at their leaders. Take a closer look. We are you! Thou art that, as they say in Sanskrit.

June 2005

Would you like the world's easiest job?

Would you care for this job?

This is one of the top positions in the country, commensurate with excellent pay, status and perks. Ah, you say: that probably means there's a lot of stress and responsibility attached. Not at all! Any idiot can do this job (and many do). Responsibility and accountability are minimal.

Qualifications: none! Didn't read much as a child, and failed to get those important pieces of paper when you left school? Not a problem. You simply apply, and after a brief but tumultuous selection process in which you pit your wits against some other contenders, you're appointed. Getting interested? We thought you might be.

The workload must be huge, surely? Again, no. This is a beautiful job. You have a place of work, yes, and there is an annual work schedule. But you are under absolutely no obligation to show up there! Take it easy, come to work whenever you like. That leaves you free to do whatever else you like doing: conduct other businesses; have affairs; hang around bars with your peers; or just do nothing.

In return you will get a world-beating pay package that includes: a handsome salary; a big car; amazing travel allowances; free security. Hey, we'll even throw in a gun in case you want to protect yourself from aggressive Kenyans.

Performance measures, appraisals, evaluations? No, no, none of that new-fangled wrong-headed modern management gibberish has ever penetrated the very thick walls of our establishment. And never will, so rest assured: no-one will be going around measuring your performance. We're all friends here!

And did we mention the clincher? Guess who sets your pay? No, no, not your boss. You don't really have a boss. There are shareholders, yes, but they don't seem to care what happens. So the person who decides what you get is...you! Isn't that just amazing? You will receive an irrevocable 5-year contract (renewable); and we are currently trying to arrange a HUGE golden handshake at the end of the term, to thank you for your hard work.

We see you are running to update your CV. But you'll need a job title before you prepare an application. This position is called Member of Parliament in the National Assembly of the Republic of Kenya. Apply within; you may be set up for life.

Jokes aside (as they never say in the august House), it's time we all got a little outraged about our MPs. The National Assembly must be one of the most colossal wastes of money known to humankind. A job that lavishes rewards for no performance can only have been designed by the job-holders themselves.

But your MP will no doubt tell you that he (he is unlikely to be a she) does Very Important Work in the hallowed chamber. Yes, issues such as monkeys harassing peasant women in the fields (forcing them to wear trousers) are regularly discussed and debated at great length. The few people who show up to work are often ready to exchange insults and blows (including the few 'shes').

These are the people who allow important bills to be passed without a quorum, and then want to convince you about their effort and endeavour. These are the people who let a dreadfully regressive and draconian bill pass under their noses without showing up at the chamber to debate it; then take to the streets protesting and showing their solidarity with heroic journalists.

If you want these people to think about any important issue, you must fund a "retreat" (from what?) to take them to Mombasa to reflect on the matter amidst the cooling ocean breezes. You must give them a ticket and hefty allowances while they're there, so that they don't have any minor financial worries to distract them while they are with you.

Having violated your trust for five years, these people now want to award themselves a generous thank-you present from you, so that you get a chance to express gratitude to them for advancing the nation during their last 60 months in office. Sorry, delete 'in office', because they were never there.

Jokes aside (because the joke's on you), why do you stand for this? Why do you accept it, tolerate it, humour it, laugh it off? Your money is being used to block the important business that would improve your life and advance your nation -- but you want to stand there laughing?

The House of Parliament is an extremely important place. It is a crucial institution in the national landscape. Contrary to what the current inhabitants might have you believe, it is not a circus tent. It is a serious place that should be populated with serious people.

The best news I heard recently concerned a poll that indicated that 90 per cent of Kenyans intend to vote out their member of parliament. If true, that is an excellent intention. The only quick way to get good performance is to penalise bad performance. The vote is the only weapon you have. Put it in your whip-hand and crack it.

September 2007

Let's pamper our MPs even more...

There seems to be a bit of noise in the country about a proposal to build a walkway connecting the Parliament Building, Continental House and County Hall at a proposed cost of Sh 61 million. This is to allow our members of parliament to cross the road with ease as they walk between their primary workplaces.

Kenyans seem a bit miffed by this, regarding it as an unnecessary extravagance at a time when the country as a whole is experiencing a recession and many Kenyans are starving for a living. But I find this reaction misplaced and misguided. I think we should be doing more for the comfort and ease of our MPs and leaders, not less.

For one thing, this thing should not be a 'walkway' at all. Let us double the cost and make it an escalator. Why do we want our leaders to be covered in sweat as they arrive in the hallowed house? Most of them are carrying a great deal of excess weight due to their status as it is; please let them cross the road in comfort.

Can Kenyans please realise that these are the top dogs of society that we are talking about? Let us not drag them down to our level, having to dodge crazed matatus, insistent beggars and other unpleasant irritants on the road. We must understand: great societies are structured for the pleasure and uplift of leaders, not the unwashed masses. I think this point is not being made often enough. Many over-educated mischief-makers are indeed making the opposite point: that we must worry unnecessarily about the common people. As many MPs can confirm, education beyond age fifteen is a waste of time anyway.

Indeed, there are many valid reasons why the almost-holy feet of MPs should never have to touch the street at all. As we know, these people have many enemies due to the weight of responsibilities that they carry on our behalf. There are many wastrels and ne'er-do-wells who are looking for every opportunity to accost parliamentarians in the street. It's a long list: political enemies; creditors; angry spouses; mistresses; former lovers; frustrated constituents; relatives seeking handouts; old schoolfriends; partners in failed ventures; barmaids; former campaign managers; future campaign managers; unpaid workers; gang leaders; auctioneers and more.

Given that list, can we please spare our elected representatives any unnecessary embarrassments and complications? Let them walk around in peace, aloof from the pollution, noise and disturbance created by the likes of you and me.

Some of you seem offended by the amount in question. But what is sixty million shillings, really? If instead it was divided equally between every Kenyan, what would we all get? Two shillings! What are you going to do with two bob? Let us be enlightened about these matters and put money where it really makes a difference. If our leaders can walk around in comfort, they will have more time to think about development and uplift for the rest of us.

There are some noisemakers who have been busy listing what else we could do with sixty million shillings. They point out, for example, that we could build a brand-new two-kilometre road in

Nairobi which would ease the traffic problem. Or that we could feed two hundred thousand starving Kenyans for a month, or resettle a few thousand internally displaced persons, blah blah blah.

Again, we are missing the point. If Nairobians are given another road, they will just rush there with their cars and jam it up in a week. If we feed starving Kenyans, they will be starving again as soon as the rains fail to come. If we resettle IDPs, they will simply offend their new neighbours again. If we educate children, they will just burn their schools down. These are not productive uses of scarce funds. Building a walkway (or rather a 'glideway') clearly is.

In fact, we should apply the same reasoning to other items of proposed expenditure, such a Sh 100 million house for the Speaker, a Sh 500 million house for the vice-president, a Sh 1 billion refurbishment of parliament chambers, etc. These are the investments we must make for the future of our children. Let us invest in the comfort, status, convenience and luxury of our leaders. When these people are freed of the stresses of daily life, they will apply their large brains to the problem of how to look after wananchi.

Look, we're never going to be world-beating in anything but running. We might as well forget about the welfare of 35 million Kenyans, and instead focus on 350. Even if we grow our economy at a phenomenal rate for the next twenty years, the income of the average Kenyan might only match that of the average South African or Egyptian. So what?

Far better to ensure that a few hundred people in the country earn world-beating salaries, enjoy the best perks and rub shoulders with the world's best. That way, Kenya can take its rightful place in the world. *Ama*?

June 2009

The Kenyan leadership quiz

Do you dream of being a leader in Kenya? Do you want to be a cabinet minister, and see that flamboyant flag fluttering on your bonnet? Perhaps a permanent secretary, in total control of thousands of minions? Do you want to see Kenyans gape at you in open-mouthed awe as you pass by? Do you wish to arrive in your constituency in a helicopter, scattering the natives as you land? Do you want people to hang on to your every word, no matter what infantile gibberish you spout? Do you want never to be held accountable for anything you say or do?

Who wouldn't? If there is a heaven on earth, leadership in Kenya is it. But we have bad news for you. There's a long list of applicants, and very few top posts to fill. The good news is that a major restructuring is rumoured to be looming, so some vacancies are likely to appear. In its newfound emphasis on merit-based recruitment and transparency, the government has announced a simple aptitude test to be taken by all applicants for top leadership positions. This short test assesses all the qualities and competencies needed by the holders of exalted office. The *Sunday Nation* managed to get its hands on an advance copy, and we publish the test exclusively in today's edition.

1. Which statement below best summarises your level of academic achievement?

a. A good bachelor's degree from a reputable local university.

b. Two undergraduate degrees, several post-graduate diplomas and a doctorate in subjects such as Cane Husbandry, or the Morphology of Esoteric Linguistic

Structures, obtained from internationally renowned institutions in the Bahamas, Tajikistan, the Outer Hebrides, etc.

c. Expelled in Standard Six for persistent delinquency.

2. To which political party do you belong?

a. The party that has stood by the same principles since independence, and which now has the most credible policies to attack poverty in the country.

b. The party that represents my tribe.

c. Whichever party is currently in power, naturally.

3. Which political figure do you most admire?

a. Graca Machel

b. Silvio Berlusconi

c. Johnnie Walker

4. Where do your children live?

a. In their home village, where they will work to bring development.

b. In Nairobi, because that's where the action (and all the money) is.

c. In Los Angeles, Sydney, Toronto and Johannesburg, because this country has no future.

5. **What, in your view, would be the most desirable signs of success in your ministry, department or parastatal?**

   a. Hard-working staff serving the needs of wananchi.

   b. Well-appointed offices and a fleet of the best limousines.

   c. An organisation teeming with all the unemployable dimwits from my home district.

6. **What is your political/economic doctrine?**

   a. Social democracy : a system that gives untrammelled freedoms and incentives to all individuals to engage with a modern economy, within a framework of human dignity and basic rights.

   b. Kenyan capitalism: those that have everything shall receive tax waivers, those that have something shall watch it trickle upwards, those that have nothing shall be asked to work harder and pay taxes on time.

   c. *Ati?*

7. **What is this country's biggest problem?**

   a. Poverty.

   b. Lack of economic growth.

   c. Busybodies and activists in the media and civil society who refuse to acknowledge the government's remarkable efforts and achievements in fighting corruption in a country that was once the most corrupt in the world and is now teaching the world how to design an anti-corruption strategy.

8. **What is the single most important goal you will set yourself as a leader in this country?**

   a. To reduce the number of people living on less than a dollar a day by half within five years.

   b. To increase my personal fortune by five times every year for five years.

   c. To ensure that Kenya hosts the Winter Olympics, a Formula One Championship, and the European Champions' League final at Kasarani within five years.

9. **What will your approach to economic planning be?**

   a. To design realistic plans that utilise local inputs and prioritise immediate growth opportunities, and require a period of austerity and constrained spending.

   b. To design grandiose recovery strategies requiring several hundred billion dollars that will be funded by development partners and Bill Gates.

   c. To open a series of numbered accounts in offshore tax havens in the name of phantom firms.

10. **What do you expect will be your catch phrase when responding to awkward questions from the media?**

   a. "Thank you for bringing this matter to my attention. As the minister in charge of this area, I am accountable to the people of Kenya. I apologise for any shortcomings in our work. I will conduct very thorough investigations into the matter. In exactly three days' time I will convene a press conference to announce what actions are being taken."

b. "I am not aware."

c. "This is an orchestrated attempt at character assassination by my political enemies and Satan-worshippers funded by foreign masters who have lost lucrative contracts due to my diligence."

11. When a foreign envoy attacks the government, how will you respond?

a. By arranging a private meeting with the person concerned to understand the situation, and then making a sober response in measured terms.

b. By characterising it as a racist and neo-colonialist attack on the innocent children of Kenya.

c. By depicting the envoy as a drunkard who is nursing a grudge against the country because he was jilted by a Kenyan woman.

12. How many days do you expect to spend out of the country in the course of your ministerial duties every month?

a. Zero - this country's problems are homegrown and require locally generated solutions. This will take all of my focused attention. I will have no time to travel.

b. 5 to 10. There is a lot to learn from the world -why reinvent the wheel? Travel broadens the mind.

c. 25 to 30. With first-class travel, the best hotels, plus thousands of dollars in per diems? Are you kidding? Shopping capitals of the world, here I come (with Mrs. Leader in tow, of course).

Scoring

Award yourself:

1 point for every '**a**' answer,
3 points for every '**b**' answer
5 points for every '**c**' answer

Tot up your total: _____ points.

Evaluation

12 - 23 points

Who do you think you are, Mwalimu Nyerere? Even Tanzania wouldn't appoint you a leader these days. Your application will be sent to Kamiti to be used for lavatorial purposes by high-net-worth prisoners.

24 - 49 points

You show a good deal of promise. However, you still lack some of the critical acumen and skills demanded by a modern Kenyan leader. You should consider spending a period of time in private business. Suitable enterprises include a law partnership, the matatu industry or international arms dealerships.

50+ points

Step forward, *Bwana Mkubwa*! Your deportment is magisterial, your wisdom inconsequential. You are free from all ethics and devoid of content. Expect to receive a call soon on your mobile phone!

February 2005

Let's just hand over power to women

"Behind every successful man is a woman" is the well-known saying. Noted wit Groucho Marx added some words to this: "Behind every successful man is a woman; behind her is his wife." That certainly rings true in Kenya...

But I would like to disagree with the original statement. I think it should say: "In front of every capable woman is a man taking all the glory." That happens to be true in my case. Much of what you read in this column on many a Sunday springs from the mind of a woman (who, worry not, is also my wife).

Let me go further. I think that if men continue to dominate the leading discourse of this country, if they continue to straddle the corridors and boardrooms of power - then we are cooked. The dire straits we find ourselves in are largely the result of masculine behaviour. Men, as a rule, do ugly things to others and to the world around them. They compete manically and brutally; they love to give orders; they are terrible at sharing power; they deplete resources; and they like simple, unambiguous solutions to everything.

Recent studies reveal that women actually outscore men in most managerial competencies. Does this surprise you? Consider that women (on average) are adept at certain things: they find a collaborative approach much easier than men do; they value and appreciate diversity; they share knowledge freely rather than hide it; they have higher emotional intelligence and sensitivity; and they see the nurturing of talent as a natural goal, rather than a grudging concession. And guess what? These are precisely the managerial attributes demanded by the new economy.

The problem is that women live in a man's world, where all the rules are set to favour men. Men call the shots, and structure society to shun and mock the women who dream of wearing the trousers. Men may appreciate the fact that women bring certain skills to the workplace, but they want women to know their place. And so they will ensure that they have a woman on their board of directors - and stop there. Or a couple of women in their top executive team - and stop there.

Political leaders? Don't even go there. Corporate man looks like a shrill feminist compared to the dinosaurs who bestride the politics of the land. But do remember what happened to the dinosaurs...

So women are far from breaking through into overall leadership, in politics or in business. But here's something that I've been noticing over the last couple of years in corporate Kenya: women are taking over middle management. Look around: women may be under-represented in the top echelons, but they are beginning to dominate the middle layers of most leading companies. I've been counting wherever I go, and I can tell you the numbers are growing fast. There is also no doubt in my mind that better companies are emerging as a result.

Management guru Tom Peters highlighted recently that in America women are starting businesses at a rate seven times higher than men. This has created an eye-popping result: the revenue from women-owned businesses in America now exceeds the GDP of Germany. Are you paying attention yet? Women of Kenya, are you going to start the businesses you've always wanted to, and run them YOUR way?

I was recently asked to give a motivational talk at a large community centre. The committee that approached me was run entirely by women. They persuaded me to do it within a few minutes of meeting me, and in a few days had designed and delivered all the promotional material. Then they got going selling the tickets. Within one week, I kid you not, they had sold out the entire auditorium. I know very well that this was less to do with me and more to do with the dedicated, concerted selling performance they put on.

Would a committee of men have achieved the same result? Forgive me for doubting it. Men would have been absorbed in protocols and hierarchies; they would have spent long hours planning rather than doing; and they would have tried to delegate all the hard work (probably to women).

We know that biologically, women are given the hardest of jobs: the rearing and nurturing of children. But it is only in a man's world that the job is trivialised and under-valued, when it is the foundation of talent in the country. And it is only in a man's world that women are deemed to be good for only the things that come before and after childbirth. But watch this space: it won't be a man's world for that much longer.

So what are we going to do with ourselves, men? Go back to the farms? No, because there won't be any women left there to do all the hard work. Perhaps we can just do the thing we are genuinely good at: watch sports! And ladies, when you do take over, remember I was on your side...

March 2009

CHAPTER FOUR
An Enterprising Nation:
Kenya's Peculiar Businesses

Kenyans are well-known for being enterprising - rapaciously so, according to our neighbours. If there's a buck to be made selling something, you can be sure a Kenyan will be selling it. Indeed, this spirit of enterprise is what sustains us: in a country of forty million people, we only provide 'proper' jobs to two million or so. There is a vast informal sector making and selling stuff against all odds and despite all the attempts of regulators and busybodies to muzzle them. And Kenya's burgeoning larger businesses, too, set a certain standard in the region.

But, make no mistake, these are all peculiar businesses! I have spent the better part of the past fifteen years working with and observing businesses large and small in Kenya. We do some very strange things in these parts - from the way we work to the protocols that govern us. This has provided me with rich material over the years with which to poke fun at chief executives, boards of directors, managers and shareholders.

In the course of thinking about this book, I came across the following scraggly hand-written sign on a fancy shop window: "This year's diaries and calendars on sale, knock-down price." In October. That's Kenyan business for you. Sadly, I have no doubt that Kenya's bargain-crazed and freebie-mad shoppers went in to enquire...

I have selected three articles to take you on a short business

*tour of Kenya. The first shows how many businesses in Kenya
are everything but what they should be - businesses! The second
focuses on the fast-spreading disease of "business-speak"; and
the third puts you in attendance at that unique event, the Kenyan
Annual General Meeting.*

The many agendas
of Kenyan business

Why aren't we producing more truly great companies? We certainly have some world-class outfits in our midst; but they are needles in the corporate haystack. There are a few corporations that produce goods and services of stellar quality, are good to their employees, run an efficient operation, and generate consistent value for their shareholders. But there are not many. Why so, when we are an unabashedly capitalist nation steeped in entrepreneurial spirit?

Many business leaders will rush forward at this point to shout about the costs of doing business, the state of the infrastructure, corruption in high places, violence in low places and the general uselessness of our politicians. Um, yes. Maybe. But that does not explain the whole picture. I think much of the blame must fall at the feet of business leaders, managers and executives. Many of those who lead us in the business world are simply too distracted to do a good job.

The outspoken economist Milton Friedman proclaimed 35 years ago that: "The business of business is business". What he meant is this: that success in business demands a single-minded and relentless focus on the task of turning a profit. Businesses exist to generate wealth for their owners; that must be their primary focus. If they do this well, the business will perform well. It will reward employees who generate value; it will create robust demand for inputs; it will supply products or services needed in the economy; and it will do all these things, in its own interest, on a sustainable, long-term basis. When businesses perform, the economy performs.

Very good. But does this happen in Kenya? I fear not. Business is used by many executives as a platform from which to do other things. There are many agendas in Kenyan business; the agenda of superior business performance is only one of them. We see this lack of focus all around us in the business world: in state corporations, in family-owned firms; even in publicly listed companies. So what are these additional agendas that so burden Kenyan business? You know them well.

Let's begin with the Politics Agenda.

Many businesses are, to their great cost, inextricably entwined with politics. Their boards are stacked with political operators; their bosses are associated with particular parties; the MD might be eyeing a parliamentary seat himself. So what happens? Funds and resources get diverted, particularly at campaign time. Large donations must be made; the company's vehicles, computers, telephones and photocopiers must be diverted for campaign use. Thriving corporations have been brought down this way.

The second distraction is the Tribal Agenda.

A Kenyan executive is not just a business professional; he or she is also a high-profile representative of a tribe. The tribe, however, does not just view the executive's career from afar with pride and benevolence. Oh, no. It's payback time! A large number of village kinsmen and idlers will bedevil this executive, seeking favours, employment, donations, introductions, etc. Long queues will form in the company's reception room. The executive's prestige in the clan is linked to the number of such favours given to tribespeople, so the pressure is intense. In return, the tribe will "protect" the executive when "political forces" try to "finish" him. Nothing to do with business, except for the cost in lost performance.

A third one: the Family Agenda.

Many Kenyan businesses originate as family concerns. Nothing wrong with that; it's the nature of business all over the world. The problem comes when people fail to distinguish between the family's interests and those of the business. It may well be to the family's benefit that all its members are kept gainfully employed; the business, however, must select its employees on merit and for their ability to deliver bottom-line performance. So when dissolute uncles and unemployable cousins are given senior positions, there is only going to be one outcome for the business: bankruptcy.

Here's another: the Perks Agenda.

Many business leaders give you the impression that they are not employed to deliver results: merely to enjoy the trappings of office. Their typical activities, therefore, consist of the following: attendance at every high-level seminar in town; endless cocktail parties; rounds on the golf course "networking" with well-connected peers; conferences on unlikely subjects in far-flung lands which allow the spouse to shop and the air-miles to accumulate nicely. All these things have only the vaguest connection to the business's performance; yet many leaders do little else. The tedious work of running the company to turn a profit is delegated to lesser mortals. The job of the leader is to hobnob with the high and mighty.

And finally, and most perilously, there is the Fraud Agenda.

Many Kenyan executives are not in business for business at all; they are there to seek opportunities to fleece shareholders and achieve overnight personal enrichment. Offshore procurement contracts, dubious tender awards, financial fiddles and the like offer ample opportunity for this. Sadly, this is not an isolated tendency. How many household business names have we seen brought down to their knees in recent years, crippled by executive greed and malpractice? How many "abuse of office" cases keep emerging in the public sector?

The one external agenda that business leaders in a poor country could legitimately preoccupy themselves with is that of social responsibility and capacity building. This is necessary in the face of government abdication; it is even in the long-term interests of shareholders. Yet this is the one agenda that is most neglected, and is least interesting for the very busy (see above) business leader.

So is it a surprise that we struggle to produce world-beating companies? We're not really running businesses; we're running tribes, families, political campaigns, personal empires and feeding troughs. That is not the stuff of which top corporations are made. Our leading firms distinguish themselves by focusing relentlessly on operations, markets, and customers. They are immersed in the task of being better then their competitors. They are wholly absorbed in the process of delivering measurable improvement in key indicators. They don't have the time or the inclination to mess about with ulterior and extraneous agendas.

We have to get serious about business performance. Great economies are built by a very simple mechanism: putting the right people in the right place to do the right job at the right time. We are too tolerant – as shareholders, directors, employees, citizens and observers – of superfluous agendas. Ethnicity, kinship, politics and merrymaking must be taken off the business plan once and for all.

May 2005

The lost art of speaking plainly

Do you understand the following sentences?

"The government is committed to developing innovative, proactive and goal-focused policies that reflect the aspirations of all Kenyans and meet the expectations of key stakeholders. We will focus on efficient and effective service delivery in an environment of transparency and accountability."

Or consider the following typical 'mission statement' from a private-sector company:

"Our mission is to be a world-class performance-based provider of leading-edge products, exceeding customer expectations and continuously enhancing shareholder value by proactively leveraging deep and diverse management skills and deploying our rich human capital base, governed by our corporate values of teamwork, excellence, integrity and innovation."

I don't know about you, but my eyes glaze over when I see or hear this stuff. What does it mean? Can you make any sense of it? It is, I'm afraid, the type of gibberish emanating from many government officials and corporate managers these days in their zeal to appear professional.

We used to worry about whether English would supplant Kiswahili, whether Sheng was a good thing, and whether our regional tongues would die out. The real danger lies elsewhere: that as we advance, we will all be overcome by a very strange language called international business-speak. This language takes over the mind in a very crafty fashion: it introduces itself while we are at school in the form of a few innocent-sounding words; it strengthens its grip at university where we realise that whole sentences can be strung together with these new words; and it finally grabs us by the lapels when we enter the world of work, when we quickly realise that our peers speak nothing else and proficiency in the language is a prerequisite for success.

By then our brains are thoroughly washed; we are unthinking robots who cannot speak or write a sentence without using words like 'state-of-the-art', 'innovative', 'proactive', 'goal-seeking' and 'people-driven.'

As our society advances, we are all embracing business-speak. It is heard in conferences, seminars and in the corridors of power. It fills our newspapers and reverberates on our radios and televisions. It is spoken in bars and cocktail parties. It is the de facto language of success. Use it, or you are a nobody.

Yet this language of so-called success is vapid and meaningless. We are all mouthing the words, having forgotten their meaning a long, long time ago. What does it mean to speak of 'excellence', for example, when each and every organisation claims to achieve it? The word refers to being pre-eminent or the most outstanding; can every company be the most outstanding? How many organisations have you come across in Kenya that can be called outstanding, even in jest? Yet 'excellence' is on every annual report and mission statement. It is so overused that it has lost its original motivational value.

As our parastatals begin their renaissance under new leadership, they are all producing visions and mission statements filled with lofty goals and noble values. Trouble is, they all look almost exactly the same! What possible value can there be in a statement about your corporation that is just like your neighbour's? How can you proclaim your uniqueness by touting a declaration that looks like it came off an assembly line?

There is a serious danger here. It is that we use the words to look and sound good, but we actually do or achieve very little. As part of our 'stakeholder management', we spew this stuff out in all directions. It makes us look like we have the right MBA degrees in our pockets. It projects a professional image. It soothes the ear of other business-speak exponents. It lulls the listener into treacherous somnolence. But it is very often a complete sham, a way of wagging the silver tongue when the pocket contains nothing.

A mea culpa is probably in order here. My profession (management consulting) bears a heavy responsibility for this state of affairs. So do the writers of business bestsellers. Many in the business thrive by introducing buzzwords, jargon and techno-speak on a regular basis. It is very often a substitute for real content, a proxy for genuinely new ideas. But the zest with which corporate titans embrace this emptiness is truly alarming.

I worry even more when I hear the language beginning to infiltrate the speeches of our cabinet ministers. These people really need to deliver results, for all our sakes. We cannot afford to let them engage in sophistry and the peddling of snake oil. We need to see them create jobs and fix roads, not brandish jargon in our faces. They need to talk less and do more.

Related to this malady is the ailment of aping pronunciation. Is there really a problem with not knowing your 'rent' from your 'lent' if you are a Kikuyu, or your 'sheep' from your 'seep' if you are a Luo, or your 'vest' from your 'west' if you are of Indian origin? Isn't all this variety what makes Kenya such an interesting place? How tedious it would be if we all sounded the same! Our diversity is our strength, and we should embrace all its faces.

Yet listen to our newscasters and TV reporters: they are engaging in very painful oral somersaults to sound westernised and modern. Some of them seem to be in serious danger of dislocating their jaws every night; such is their keenness to astound us with their vocal gymnastics. Who is training these people in such artifice? One appreciates the need for a certain standardisation, but our reporters' efforts are comical at best. Yet, rather than laughing at them, our youngsters imitate them. We seem to be raising a generation that uses words it doesn't comprehend and makes sounds no-one understands. A modern Tower of Babel, indeed!

How I long for an era of plain speaking, when people will say what they think and say it without unnecessary adornment! When we will begin without initiating, and end without terminating. When we will pay without disbursing, and hasten without expediting. When we will help without facilitating, and will be aware without taking cognisance. How much more appealing our speech and writing will be then! People will use the words they like and understand, not the ones they have to be seen using.

By engaging in contrivance, we are evading reality. We are placing a veil over our real problems. We are hiding our failures behind silly words and empty phrases. We are displaying our insecurity about our heritage by talking like parrots. Letting our words reflect our true selves may be a first step towards reclaiming our dignity.

June 2003

Music, lights, freebies: welcome to the Kenyan AGM

The amazing success of the Safaricom IPO confirms that we are on our way to becoming a shareholder democracy, does it not? Hundreds of thousands of new shareholders have been brought into the bosom of capitalism, and are basking in the promise of the new wealth that will follow - yes?

Anyone who thinks we are en route to a mass-capitalist society needs to visit the Annual General Meeting of any listed company to check up on this. My work takes me to quite a few, and I rarely leave inspired about the future.

People flock in their thousands to the bigger companies' AGMs. By observation, many come from rural outposts, using the meeting as a reason to come to the capital city. Most, I am afraid to report, haven't the faintest clue what they are there to do, or indeed what "their" company does. They are simply like children at the circus, waiting for the show to begin.

And a show it is. Many companies now organise dancing and singing troupes to perform at AGMs, thereby accepting that there is no serious business to be conducted there. They give out freebie packs - to much pandemonium. I have often heard shareholders (and even financial journalists) rating companies according to the quality of the free lunch provided.

Once the business of discussing the company's Annual Report is underway, a few questions will indeed be asked by shareholders - mostly by the half-dozen or so "career shareholders" we have in this country who are found at each and every public AGM and who invariably try to impress the assembly with predictable and banal questions.

When the average shareholder does get to ask a question, it will be along the lines of: "Why can't this meeting begin at 11:00 am instead of 2:00 pm, to allow us to use the afternoon for other things?" Or "Why didn't we begin this meeting with a prayer to bless the proceedings?" Or "I demand that this company publishes the names of all employees so that we can confirm that the country's eight provinces are represented equally." Heaven help us.

Because shareholders behave like children, they are treated as such by chairmen and directors. The meeting is tightly scripted; questions are given short shrift, whether important or not; and the major issues facing the company are almost NEVER discussed. The company's competitive edge; its penetration of regional markets; the trends in its cash management; the turnover in senior management: I have yet to attend an AGM where questions about such issues are raised.

If even ten million Kenyans buy a few shares in a few companies, we will not become a knowledgeable shareholder economy. In fact, the more the shareholders out there, the more vulnerable they are to criminal manipulation by stockbrokers, who herd these people out of the villages with the contents of their freshly emptied mattresses and lure them into putting their life savings into whichever company the stockbroker is promoting that week. Like sheep being taken for fleecing.

If you want to see the tragedy that unfolds, go and look at the queues outside the offices of defunct stockbrokers. Look at the distress on the faces of the assembled, as it sinks in that ten years of hard saving may have disappeared in the blink of an eye. We are not creating shareholder democracy here, we are creating a 'karata' economy where a few schemers dupe millions of suckers.

A company succeeds because it has a robust business model, determined leadership and a long record of innovation. Business is not a street-corner card game. If a company is going to make anyone any real money, it will happen over a long period - and only if the company manages to sustain its market leadership in the face of the very intense competition to come.

I repeat what I have written many times before: money is not made in the crowd. If you are standing in a queue thinking you'll be rich just by doing what everyone else is doing, think again. The chances are, some huckster is lining you up for fleecing.

July 2008

CHAPTER FIVE
Ordinary people, peculiar lives

The most fun to be had is in observing Kenyans conduct the business of ordinary living. Over the years, I have found myself intrigued by so many things.

Why, for example, do Kenyans watch others jumping queues ahead of them - but never object? Why do they allow "overlappers" on the roads to cut in ahead of them? Why don't they say anything to bus drivers who drive at racing-car speeds, taking them to near-certain death? Why do foreign ambassadors behave like hectoring headmasters addressing retarded children? Why are funerals used for politicking, in the presence of weeping relatives?

Why do cyclists wear black at night and not bother to invest in cheap lights and reflectors? Why is it socially acceptable to become obese once you've made some money? Why do people who were engineers or ambassadors insist on being called by those titles decades after they have stopped being active in those occupations? Why is being a single mother so commonplace?

Why is roasted meat the limit of our culinary ambitions? Why do Kenyans grow up, study, work and die in ethnic enclaves? Why are we so obsessed with owning land? Why are Kenyan academics so irredeemably pompous? Why don't we have a national dress? Why do people rush into a lift before those inside can get out? Why do slow drivers all stick to the fast lane on highways? Why do church leaders invariably ask politicians present to "address the congregation", knowing full well that un-Christian sentiments are about to be expressed?

I have been chronicling these peculiarities of ordinary Kenyan life since 2003. The next set of articles provides a flavour, looking at our daily corruptions; our penchant for mimicry; our famous traffic jams; our propensity for nostalgia; our never-changing daily headlines; the way we lead our love lives; the peculiarities of our famous coastline; and another quiz on our national and personal priorities. I conclude with two pieces that set to record our most obvious common peculiarities.

Roll up, roll up:
everything is for sale in Kenya

Britain was once called a nation of shopkeepers. If so, then Kenya can only be a nation of hawkers, vendors, and peddlers. Not to mention hucksters and spivs. For everything is on sale in Kenya. I'm not referring to the normal range of goods and services. In Kenya, you can buy anything – including things that should never be on the market in the first place.

For a start, democracy is up for sale. Do you want to become an MP? No problem. Some hundred-shilling-note handouts, a few T-shirts and caps and the promise of *nyama choma* can buy you the post. That's the price attached to the position by the average impoverished Kenyan voter.

Do you want government to do something for you? A juicy contract, some influence in the right places? No problem, it's all available - at a range of prices. A few deposits in offshore accounts, some wining and dining and hey presto! Government is yours. And the wonderful thing is, very often you don't even have to supply anything! Can there be a better deal than that? What a place in which to do business! Come one, come all.

So what's new, you say? We know government is on sale. If only we could get rid of these swindlers masquerading as leaders, we would be fine. But would we really? I'm afraid the rot goes much deeper, dear reader. The disease is in all of us. We're all buyers and sellers in The Great Kenya Sale.

What do our corporate managers and professionals sell? The shampoos they make and the services they offer? Yes indeed, but a lot more besides. Hefty procurement contracts are up for sale – just grease the right palms, and you could be supplying shoddy goods at showcase prices for years to come. Legal judgements can be auctioned to the highest bidder – just arrange a quiet handover in a dimly lit car park. Your opponents' lawyers are up for sale – just talk to them about ruining their client's case. Cooking your books? Worry not, auditors can be found to help you bake the final dish to perfection.

Proud companies providing employment to thousands don't just sell their products – their managers and directors are often up for sale, too. They will loot it dry and leave a withered shell. They will put families out on the street. Nothing personal, just business. Managers got rich, the economy got poorer. A profitable day's work for those who know how.

Looking for publicity? Need to put your nasty company in a favourable light? Or perhaps have an investigation lead nowhere? No problem, journalists can be found to help you do all that, for very little outlay. Perhaps you want your property valued highly as collateral for a bank loan? Don't worry, the bank's own valuer will do the needful – for a share of the difference.

Our learned academics also have stalls laid out in this bazaar. Need a study done to show that your project will have minimal environmental impact? Don't fret, our professors, too, have a taste for the finer things in life. And a consultant can undoubtedly be found to put a sparkling sheen on the economic projections. Take your time to browse carefully when visiting this *soko* of ours – most things are available.

Security is for sale, of course – guards, fences, and alarms.

But so is insecurity. Need to organise a break-in? Start a riot? Execute a business rival? You can pay the same guards to look the other way. Pay some idlers to start stoning cars. Hire guns from wayward policemen. Get people to work on both sides of the law, simultaneously.

The beauty of the country is up for sale. Its mountains and its beaches, its wildlife and its trees – all carry a price tag. Can you afford it? Step forward. We will allow you to ruin coral reefs, pollute rivers and lakes, and fence off as many thousands of acres as you want. We even want to allow you to chase after our animals in four-wheel drive cars and shoot them dead – just for the thrill of the chase, just to indulge the sickness in your soul that wants to take an innocent life. We have no problem with that – the animals of earth are just goods on a shelf to us: pay your money and start shooting.

Are you wondering what happened to traditional African values like sharing and hospitality? Why, they went in a special clearance sale years ago! We exchanged them for more modern merchandise: individuality, greed and personal gain. What happened to the rich languages we were going to teach our children? We traded them in for English – much better to help the kids make it in life, don't you think? Dholuo or Punjabi doesn't really help you out there on the world commercial stage, after all. Sell it for a few burgers and fries (soda not included); that's all a language is worth these days.

Sex has always been on sale – but not just on the streets of shame. It sells in the boardrooms and bedrooms of the high and mighty, too. Having a mistress is a sign of affluence and status; being one is an honourable vocation these days. Upmarket apartments, glittering jewels and foreign trips are the price; family values are the cost.

Can't have children, and can't accept it as God's wish? No problem, with the right help, it can become God's miracle. Little babies are on sale too, and you don't even have to feel any guilt, because God Almighty will be roped in to underwrite the transaction. Have you run a once-vibrant city into the ground? Not a setback at all: prayers are available for cash, to help you fool all the people all the time. Looking for prime land for your temple? No problem, a tycoon will grab you some to cleanse his sins. In Kenya, even God is for sale, retailed by his own messengers for a few pieces of presidential-portrait silver.

But you don't do any of that, do you? It's those other people, isn't it? Your personal virtue is intact, is it not? Until someone asks you to pay cash and avoid VAT, that is. Until someone shows you a pirated CD at a third the cost of the original, that is. Until you spot an opportunity to fiddle your expense claims, that is. Until you start running a private business using your employer's facilities, that is. Until the smallest temptation tickles your nose, that is. Then your personal virtue is well and truly up for sale, at bargain prices.

Yes, we're open for business in Kenya. We're all punters in the sale of the century. Come and see the free market go to places it's never been before. Listen to those cash tills ring - that's the real music of the land! Roll up, roll up, place your bids and carry away your goods. You'll be surprised at the range of merchandise and the throw away prices. No credit, mind – nobody can be trusted here. Cash upfront (no VAT), for the soul of a nation.

September 2004

Why are we mimics in everything we do?

Oh, colonisation! We're still paying a heavy price, after all these years. We seem unable to move on, leave our history behind us and just get on with things. I am worried about the colonisation of our minds, which proceeds apace.

We all watch the military march-pasts when the President is officiating at a function. We all see how our boys walk like stiff clockwork soldiers, and how they twist their necks at a dangerous angle to look at the dignitaries as they walk past, whilst maintaining that ridiculous forward-march gait. We see it, but do we ask ourselves: who taught them that? Why do they still do it that way? Is our idea of martial discipline still rooted in the colonial experience? Should we, by now, not have developed our own practices, our own codes, our own rituals?

Why do our worthy judges still look like Christmas decorations, wearing those amazingly comical blonde wigs? Why is a practice that emerged from England of centuries past still enforced in a modern African nation? Why do these people address each other as 'lordships' and 'learned friends'? When will we rid ourselves of this archaic pomposity?

Why is the Speaker of the 'august' House dressed like a cartoon character? Why does he not allow any of his parliamentarians to wear local garb? Is the suit and tie still the only hallmark of professionalism and seriousness that we can imagine in a hot African republic? And why do those people in there all applaud with their feet, like overexcited little children?

Oh, those Brits left an indelible impression on our minds. And it goes to the heart of our identity as a nation. Who are we, and what do we stand for? How can we possibly tell, clothed in alien attire and steeped in outlandish rituals? And how can we become something different, something better and something authentic when we have not been able to shed the skins given to us by our conquerors?

It goes beyond clothing and ritual, this identity problem. Our religions, too, did not originate in our own lands. They came from the hallowed soils of old Judea, from the minarets of Arabia, and from the temples of ancient India. They are received religions, and we received them without question. They are not the only doctrines we import. Every year, we are forced to recite the fiscal and monetary mantras of the high priests from the World Bank and IMF. If we sing in tune and don't go off-key, a collection plate is passed round to raise some "development assistance" for us.

In our offices and boardrooms, we worship something called "best practice": the business processes and systems of other countries. We follow these things with religious intensity, because we have no business models to call our own. Our indigenous business successes are few and far between; multinationals clearly set the pace, and that is where we all wish to work. Why hurt yourself trying to think differently when these things are tried and tested, are proven on the international stage? Why, as we often say to ourselves, reinvent the wheel?

And when we relax, what do we like to do? Watch the overcooked sexual intrigues and marital discord of Mexicans and Americans in those appalling soap operas that are dumped on us and always race to the very top of our viewing charts. Or we sit in large groups in bars watching the latest battles between Chelsea, Real Madrid and AC Milan. When we read (which isn't often) we read the pulp offerings of John Grisham and Jackie Collins (with baffling pride).

Have we not become what another novelist, the acerbic V. S. Naipaul, unkindly called "mimic men" – desperately trying to copy the successes of foreigners without any real base of authenticity? But then he himself abandoned his third-world birthplace, Trinidad, at the first opportunity (and used the comfortable base of England to nurture his undoubted literary talent) so he is not perhaps our best guide in the matter.

The crux of the matter is this: no one makes it by simply copying. Cultures and practices evolve in specific settings; they are the products of local forces and local conditions. When we assume, wholesale and without question, the practices that evolved elsewhere, we are doing ourselves no favours. Best practice does not push the curve out. Accepting the wheel as the only means of locomotion keeps us from looking beyond the current reality. The Wright Brothers reinvented the wheel – they added wings to it and created the airplane! If we limit our thoughts and ideas to what we have read and received, when will we generate original ideas for others to copy?

This is not an argument for being static; it is not a paean to a pre-colonial past. Culture is dynamic, and must absorb all influences and grow in all directions. But it must have a foundation, an authentic core to call its own. A *"mitumba"* culture that happily embraces the cast-offs of others will always be second-best. The Japanese and Koreans did not get to world product leadership by mimicking western business practices; they developed their own, based on their particular view of the world. Mahatma Gandhi did not kick the British out of India by copying their methods or playing by their rules; he introduced them to the very Indian concept of non-violent resistance.

When we look for it, authenticity is all around us. We are entirely capable of designing our own attire, writing our own books and developing our own arts. We have entrepreneurs who could refine their own business models to great effect. We have scientists with a deep understanding of local conditions who can devise excellent technologies, cures and solutions. What we don't have is the vision to get behind these people, to back them and encourage them. Instead, we mock and jeer at them. When I was at school, "native!" was the greatest insult that could be aimed at one's fellow Kenyans.

This is a failure in all of us. When we fail to take someone seriously because they aren't wearing a western suit, we are jeering at ourselves. When we stick to the tired norms of decades past, we are condemning our own ability to develop. When we reject a business idea because it isn't expressed in PowerPoint, we are putting our own limitations on display.

When we learn to value our own authentically generated ideas and initiatives, we will learn to build a cultural core that we can call our own. Then we will be able to assimilate the best from the rest of the world, safe in the knowledge that we are using foreign ideas to grow and improve ourselves, not to stifle our own creativity and deaden our own minds. Until that time comes, we are dealing in counterfeit development.

April 2005

A discussion in a traffic jam

Greetings, fellow motorists. We appear to be in a traffic jam. Cars ahead, cars behind. Nowhere to go, nothing to do but wait. Perhaps we can have a little discussion as we sit immobile, to help pass the time?

We all agree, I'm sure, that the main roads of Nairobi at rush hour are no place to be. At 8 in the morning, the queue on Argwings Kodhek Road stretches from the Nairobi Hospital all the way back to Lavington. If you have the misfortune to be on Thika Road at the same time, you will be part of a line that goes from Pangani to Ruaraka – a distance of many, many kilometres. And heaven help you if you happen to be coming in from JKIA during the evening rush hour: prepare to join your brethren in silent torment on Mombasa Road.

So we have hundreds of thousands of people simply stuck in their cars, staring into space. Who benefits? Certainly the petroleum firms; perhaps the FM radio stations. For everyone else, it is time squandered. Employees turn up late at work. Important meetings fail to kick off on time. People seethe and stir restlessly in their hot vehicles, their moods worsening by the minute. Productivity undoubtedly suffers. Many countries measure the cost of lateness in billions of dollars.

But let's leave all that heavy stuff aside. Here we all are in a jam, and it helps to have a meditative frame of mind and to sink into deep contemplation during the many otherwise pointless hours you are about to spend behind the wheel. If you have this capacity, you may want to reflect on what is causing this gridlock, and what we should do about it.

Ah, I see a road planner in the brown hatchback over there. He is saying that this is simply a problem of design and capacity. Our old-fashioned radial city networks are just not equipped to deal with the hundreds of thousands of vehicles that are now piling onto the roads. They were designed for a gentler age. The answer, the planner proclaims, is to build all the 'bypasses' his department keeps talking about, so that Nairobians can get from Lavington to the airport, say, or from Loresho to Thika Road, without having to go anywhere near the city centre. Bypasses are used all over the world for precisely this reason.

But wait, we have a behavioural scientist in the pink Beetle over there. She is telling us that it is bad road behaviour that makes the traffic jams so awful. It is because we have little knowledge of the Highway Code, and even less of personal ethical codes, that we routinely cross lanes, drive into oncoming traffic and do other moronic things. It is because we place no emphasis on proper behaviour that we allow mentally disturbed people to become drivers of public vehicles.

If behaviour is the problem, then what is needed is a national good driving campaign. Campaigns work. They instil peer pressure and promote good values. They place shame and fear of discredit in the hearts of miscreants. A good driving campaign would not even lack funding: a whole range of private-sector players can be gathered to back it: petroleum firms; tyre manufacturers; vehicle sellers. We also need to get very serious about penalties for bad offences: impounding vehicles and banning drivers are measures found in every civilised country.

Both these approaches have great merit, and both would produce results. But there is a fundamental issue that they do not address, and it is this: why do we have so many cars on the roads? Why do we make it so easy to own, maintain and run a vehicle?

Now hang on, I hear the gentleman in the red Toyota shouting. Isn't the right to drive a car inalienable? Kenyans need to have the freedom to drive to wherever they want. The arteries of the economy run this way. Why would you want to mess around with it? Your point is made, sir – please get down from the roof of your vehicle.

The smart young economist in the Subaru behind you has a ready answer. Yes, you should have the freedom to own a car and drive it – provided you are paying the cost of that activity in full. Listen to her: she's saying something about 'externalities' – activities that place costs on others. When you pay a pittance for that rust-bucket from Dubai, fuel it up and put it on the road, you are placing many involuntary costs on society.

For one thing, you are adding to the congestion problem. For another, your aged engine is sending toxic fumes into everyone's nostrils. However, unless you are forced to bear these costs yourself, you will not be deterred. We are, in effect, allowing an activity to take place at less than its true cost. Over-consumption naturally ensues. The result you know about: gridlock.

If individuals face the true costs of an activity, they make the correct economic decisions. How can this be done? One way is simply to impose higher taxes on vehicles. Oops, please stop hooting all at once. Cars should not cost more, you're all shouting. They're already 'too' expensive. But those *mitumba* imports are certainly not too pricey – if anything, their true cost is not reflected at all. Does higher duty on aged imports not make sense? Alternatively, we could simply ban cars that are more than an agreed number of years old. We've started to do this, but clearly haven't gone far enough.

Perhaps the tax should come in the form of higher fuel taxes? Oh dear, please stop hooting again. It doesn't help this discussion. But you have a point: that is a sweeping measure that will make all road travel more expensive and make our economy even more 'high-cost' than it already is.

Could we look at what other countries do? You sir, in the BMW: you look well travelled and seem to feed well on per diems from your employer. What can you tell us? Congestion charges? Ah, yes. London's experiment with a charge for entering the inner city during peak hours is something of a success: peak traffic has been brought under control using a hefty £8 (Sh 1,000) daily charge. Singapore? Yes, their electronic road pricing system has successfully regulated traffic flows for many years. Also, many countries require cars over a certain age to pass an annual test for roadworthiness.

Can we agree with the lady economist that we are in this jam because we have made driving in Kenya a free-for-all- low entry costs, freedom to drive at any time at the same cost, freedom to pollute and congest? That if we found intelligent ways of incorporating the true costs of the activity we would solve the problem? No? I see you all settling back into your seats. It is true that none of us have the individual incentive to crack this one. That is why a higher agency is needed. I believe other countries call this agency 'government'.

Anyway, get comfortable, start flipping FM channels. We'll all be here for a long time.

March 2006

Time to leave the past behind

Remember the seventies? Ah, glory days! The streets were clean, and there was always parking to be found. The town and city councils actually did what we paid them to do. Nairobi had mayors who were not drawn from the criminal or professional comedian classes. There were streetlights everywhere, and they actually worked. You could walk around in Nairobi after dark. Civil servants took some pride in their work, and even smiled at you as they served you. Doctors did not kill you, and judges did not sell you out.

A bag of chips cost a couple of shillings. Chips shops were clean and hygienic, and parents went there with their children. You could eat heartily for ten bob. There were only two brands of toothpaste, and we didn't need any more. At breakfast we chose between Cornflakes and Weetabix, and never felt deprived. All children carried the same green canvas schoolbag. You could buy twenty Black Pussycats for a shilling. If you don't know what a Black Pussycat is; well, you had to be there.

We had real roads. My uncle, one of those 'flying Sikhs', could get you to Mombasa in under five hours without involving aircraft. The Safari Rally was always held at Easter, and everyone in Kenya followed it. Tens of thousands lined the route, and top international teams flew in with helicopters to thrill us. The world loved coming to Kenya, and we loved it to come.

Everyone left their gate and their front door wide open. You dialled a number using a dial (like it says), and your line never went dead. If you called 999, someone actually answered. We looked up to, and trusted, our politicians. You could drink the water straight from the tap, and it was virtually free. Even the smallest garden contained at least two fruit trees. Dozens of children gathered in the one house with a TV set at 5.35pm every weekday, to watch the one cartoon show.

The economy was booming. We enjoyed double-digit growth, routinely. The state coffers were full, and no one stole the money. Businesses were stable. Employees were loyal to one company for most of their lives. Farmers were able to market their produce and get a fair price.

Cut! That was a movie I directed, and just like in a movie, I chose every scene very carefully. Take off those rose-tinted glasses, and take another look. Here are the scenes your director left out.

Those politicians you trusted were busy dividing the country amongst themselves, tens of thousands of acres at a time. The people who raised awkward questions were picked up at midnight, and their remains were often found at remote hillsides. Journalists lived in fear, and knew which line could not be crossed.

Children may have all had the same bags, but they also had the same teachers; teachers who beat them with sticks for not doing their homework. There was only one TV station, the one and only Voice of Kenya, and it broadcast what it was told to. Often it didn't: the sign saying "normal service will be resumed as soon as possible" was one of the most frequent things on screen, accompanied by the same maddening tunes. The TV came to life at 5.30pm, and died after six hours.

There was no internet. To research this column, I would have had to trudge from library to library and still would not have got what I needed. When you sent an urgent business letter, you sat back and waited for three weeks before expecting an answer. An international telephone call cost a serious chunk of a good salary. At one stage, you could buy any car you wanted, as long as it was a Datsun 'Debe' pickup. Every driving school had a fleet of them when I was passing my test – there was nothing else available.

Those legendary businesses of yore? They were monopolies, my friend. They had no competitors, and no reason to treat their customers as beggars, let alone kings. Customer service was a glare followed by studied indifference. Quality was what the company wanted it to be; prices were controlled; tariffs protected our industries. So how many decisions did a CEO have to make?

The booming economy? A few dozen people controlled everything. We were awash in coffee money, caused by an unusual series of frosts in Brazil. We squandered the takings, and built nothing for the future. We didn't cause the good times, but we sure as hell made sure the bad times were here to stay (they never left).

We all do this. We hark back to the good old days, forgetting they didn't feel that good at the time. We keep thinking things were better, a form of selective amnesia that allows us to remember what we choose to. The problem comes when we keep trying to recreate the conditions of yesteryear, when they really have no place in the future.

"We can draw lessons from the past", said Lyndon Johnson, 'but we cannot live in it." This lesson should be heeded by many a group of Kenyans. One such group is busy trying to recreate a Kenya in which chiefs ruled with whips and the average *mwananchi* knew his place. When low interest rates and high exchange rates were good for all. When monolithic marketing organisations handled all the produce of an industry, with farmers having no choice in the matter. When no one messed with cops and spooks.

Another group harks even further back, to an idyllic Kenya that teemed with wildlife, and where a settler was master of all that he could see. These are the very people today who live in enclaves with high walls to shut out a harsh modernity. They are the ones who will resist even the building of a road close to their rural lands - because the traffic would become unbearable, darling.

Get over it, guys. There are thirty-five-million-plus Kenyans, and this is their country as much as anyone else's. The days of keeping people in their place and rigging the rules to cater for a chosen few are long gone, and rightly so. If we don't create an inclusive economy that gives everyone a real stake in it soon, then a past is all we'll have.

There is a soon-to-be Kenya of wireless broadband and virtual corporations, where a returning diaspora will bring world-class skills. A Kenya sitting amidst vicious global competition where those who blink are history. A Kenya whose future lies in the widespread acquisition of skills and knowledge, and where vast tracts of land are an irrelevance.

The world is as we see it today. There is a future we must prepare for. Looking back with faulty memories and rheumy eyes is the last thing we need. We must look at where we're going, not at the rear view mirror. Looking forward will take all our attention, and all our insight.

I'll leave you with an evocative line by writer Sean Stewart: "The present is a rope stretched over the past. The secret to walking it is: you never look down."

April 2006

Our never-changing headlines

What changes will next year bring to Kenya? Will life get better or worse? Will it all be very dull, or unbearably exciting? To answer your questions, I decided to dust off my very reliable crystal ball (made from Kitengela glass) and took a look at the headlines and stories the *Nation* will deliver to you next year. Being a prophet in Kenya is easy, because nothing ever changes. A good editor could probably write next year's headlines over the Christmas holidays, because there are things you just know are going to happen. Again. Here's a sample of perennial stories.

GOVERNMENT CALLS FOR FAMINE AID
The government yesterday issued an urgent appeal for relief aid to address the emergency famine situation affecting many remote parts of the country. Cabinet ministers called development partners to a special banquet meeting at a five-star hotel in Nairobi, owned by one of the ministers. After a five-course meal and entertainment by traditional dancers, ministers described the drought prevailing in most parts of the country as entirely unexpected. Hundreds of thousands are at risk unless food aid is provided rapidly. After coffee and biscuits were served, the donors promised to organise an emergency fund.

PARTIES SPLIT AFTER CONTROVERSIAL NOMINATIONS EXERCISE
Every major political party announced splits and the formation of new offshoots after nominations were held countrywide. Members of the ruling Narc party split into Narc (K) and Narc (Fresh). Leaders of the new splinter group took to the streets demanding immediate registration of their party and taunting

r former allies that the 'K' in Narc (K) stands for 'Kumbafu'. eanwhile, the key losers in the ODM poll announced the ormation of a new group, the Orangest Most Democratic Movement (OMDM), which was registered on the day of application. Ford Kenya also announced that it was splitting into three parties: Ford Bungoma, Ford Kakamega and Ford Busia, in order to provide more party posts and greater flexibility in joining post-election coalitions.

NEW PARTY BUILDING COLLAPSES DURING MEETING

The new building housing the recently created Narc-Orange Multiparty Alliance for the Resuscitation of Kenya (NOMARK) collapsed at 4.00 am this morning as party leaders were discussing strategies for the forthcoming national polls. The building, which was inaugurated just a week ago, is suspected to have been built with shoddy materials and without any architectural plan by a company associated with the party's treasurer. He was not present at the meeting and has not answered the *Nation's* calls. Officials present all sustained injuries, with the exception of the chairman who had gone out to the garden to answer a call of nature.

TRAFFIC POLICE LAUNCH NEW CAMPAIGN

Hundreds of unsuspecting motorists were arrested yesterday as traffic police launched a new campaign to test the roadworthiness of vehicles. The campaign, unleashed without warning, aims to check that the following new requirements are being met by motorists: valid permits for car radios and iPods; approved rubber floor mats for every passenger; a separate jack for every wheel (including the spare); two towing ropes (front and back); and a certified air freshener. Statistics showed that all cars checked on the first day of the campaign failed to meet the requirements, including two police vehicles. Dozens of bitterly complaining drivers were taken to the cells.

CITY HALL RANSACKED

Thieves struck again at the Nairobi City Hall in the small hours of the morning and took away all the computers, chairs, tables, curtains, light fittings, and toilet-seat covers in the building. Witnesses said that the stolen goods were loaded onto twelve large lorries over several hours. City Hall guards posted at the building said they were discussing politics and saw or heard nothing. City fathers ruled out an inside job, saying: "This thing was executed too effectively and smoothly to have been done by our people."

KENYANS ABROAD IN WITHERING CRITIQUE OF HOMELAND

Kenyans in Diaspora yesterday issued a damning assessment of the state of their home country. Members of Tumetoroka Kenya Kabisa (TKK), an umbrella body claiming to represent 18 million Kenyans living in 172 countries, met at an international conference in Boston, USA and decried the state of modern Kenya, noting the lack of a subway system, a work ethic, January sales and McDonald's hamburgers. They also renewed their call for legislation to enact dual nationality for Kenyans without further delay.

OIL: FIRMS TIE UP DEAL

Following last week's confirmation that huge oil fields exist off the Kenyan coast, major players moved quickly to tie up rights to the bonanza. A new entity, Angloberg International, has been given exclusive rights to the oil fields and has finalised a deal with a consortium of international oil firms to undertake the drilling. The principals behind Angloberg remain unknown, but government officials said yesterday that they were known only by acronyms so that they could protect the country's newfound wealth on behalf of all Kenyans.

TOP COMPANIES FETED IN ANNUAL AWARDS CEREMONY

The region's top companies were rewarded for their exemplary performance in a glittering ceremony conducted in Nairobi, covered live by NTV. Awards were given out for Most Handsome CEO, Best Head Office Reception Area, Best Retrenchment Package, and Most Aged Board of Directors. All awards were received by the winners in person, except for the Most Outsourced Corporation prize which was collected by the winning company's management consultants.

December 2006

You're being taken for a ride, ladies

I last wrote about Valentine's Day back in 2004. Every year since, I have resisted the temptation to rant again about this imbecilic celebration. This year, I'm unable to stop myself.

You're being taken for a ride, ladies. First, a reminder of why I was agitated three years ago. The loser, I wrote then, is love itself:

> "If I believed that Valentine's Day is merely a spontaneous expression of young and fervent love, I would be all for it. But it is not. It is one of the most vivid examples of spending created not by a genuine human emotion, but by extremely powerful brainwashing. Who does this indoctrination? There is no conspiracy afoot, no committee of marketing master brains who sit down and plot the whole thing. No, the Valentine global marketing machine is made up of disparate little components, manufacturers, retailers, and advertisers all united in a common purpose: to part the fool from his money."

Not much has changed since then; if anything, things have only gotten worse. Fools and money are being separated with remarkable ease. Estimates suggest that America spent US$ 17 billion celebrating "Valentine love" earlier this week. That's somewhat more than our total annual GDP in this country. In addition, we're told that the average spend per American consumer was in the region of US$ 120 – or a cool 8,400 bob to you and me. Looking through the papers on February 14, it was apparent that the Valentine sales machine is in overdrive here in Kenya, too.

Everyone, it seems, is in on the act: restaurants (overpriced dinners à deux); booze shops (to ease the journey to home base); hotels (stay the night to practice true love); florists and chocolate-sellers (for that short-lived gift); jewellers (for something that lasts a little longer); lingerie shops (to package your payback); mobile-phone companies (send your inane messages at a discount); card-sellers (why think, when a manufactured message is available); radio stations (engage in asinine phone-ins); even newspapers (put your love in print).

But I have to ask: where are the rest of our Kenyan companies? Why are you not partaking in the bonanza? Banks: why not provide a special loan for our cash-strapped males – give your love-squeeze a wonderful day, pay in easy instalments over 12 months? Insurance companies: offer a great product ('jilt protection cover') for those who invest in presents but fail to score. Hospitals: why not offer a unique package that gives discounted treatment for sexually transmitted diseases every March? The sky's the limit, Business Kenya. And best of all, it's not about the money at all – it's all in the name of love.

Perhaps the most honest advert for Valentine's Day was found in the form of a full-page colour advert in the press on 14th February. It was for...condoms. Now we're getting to the point about which kind of love is being celebrated.

What leaves me amazed every year is how our womenfolk get so easily led on by male admirers and male marketers. The female of our species is generally known to be more discerning, more

116

prudent and more sensible than the male. But throw some fancy flowers and expensive wine at her and it appears she's willing to throw good sense to the four winds.

Why are you letting Adam off the love hook so easily, Eve? You allow him to prove his love for just ONE DAY, and think you're getting a great deal? Baubles and bombast on February 14, and after that the man is allowed to relax and do the indifference thing for the rest of the year. Who thought up this remarkable scheme in the first place? Um, that would be a man, ladies. No woman could have devised this. But most have fallen for it.

It seems all you want is a card with an inscription that he didn't write; a fancy meal that he didn't cook; a gift that he didn't pick; and a rose that he didn't grow. And you want all of this irrelevance in public, on show, on your desk and in full view of the envious glances of all the other women who want the same thing. If that's all you want, then that's certainly all you'll get.

I repeat what I wrote in 2004: "The Valentine phenomenon is love commodified. It is love traded in tawdry bazaars. It is love abridged. It is 'me-too' love. It is a non-event in the unfolding journey that is real love. Real love is a quiet kindness stretched out over a lifetime. It is a habit, not an event."

I hate repeating myself. But you're being taken for a ride, ladies.

February 2007

Time to stop singing 'Malaika'

I have a lifelong love affair with Kenya's coastline. Our great ocean exerts an irresistible romantic pull on me. No matter how many other great seas I visit, I invariably return to the warmest embrace of them all: the Indian Ocean. Much of the money I make in this life is spent sitting at the feet of my oldest love.

As I spend my money at this most beautiful of places, I sit and observe how others spend theirs. And of late, I have felt a great unease about our coast, its economy and its people. My most recent sojourn was not a pleasant time to be on Kenya's coast. The empty hotels and beaches, the forlorn restaurants, the desperate-looking hawkers and taxi-drivers: all told the story of an industry that has once again been laid to waste as its customers desert it in fear.

If you walk along any of our popular beaches - Bamburi, Nyali, Shanzu, Watamu, Diani - you cannot fail to notice several related phenomena. The first will be the number of couples of mixed race - black and white, mostly - that you will come across. Nothing wrong with that, of course, but for one thing. The white faces will almost invariably be old and haggard; the black ones young and fresh.

Fat old men in their sixties (mostly German, for some reason) will be holding hands with slim young African girls who could be their grand-daughters. Withered old crones will be kissing taut young Kenyan men with sculpted musculature. These ill-matched couples are not thrown together by love or affection. Their bond is economic. One side of the transaction is buying the services, the attention and the presence of the other.

The buyer knows in his or her heart that the seller feels nothing other than revulsion. The seller knows that the buyer is reliving a fantasy, chasing a youth that is long gone. Neither gets any lasting satisfaction from the sale; neither obtains any long-term gain. But both carry on trading, as they have always done for decades on these sandy beaches of ours. Only the faces change.

Phenomenon number two: you cannot walk on a beach, any beach, without being accosted by hordes of desperate people trying to sell you things. What never changes is what they offer: crudely carved key-chains and statuettes; trips to the reef in very dodgy, decrepit glass-bottomed boats; massages delivered by untutored hands in unsavoury settings. There are hardly any buyers for any of this stuff; there are always dozens of sellers. And, as the beaches have emptied in recent months, the desperation on the faces of the hawkers is distressing to see.

The third phenomenon: walk into the average beach hotel, and you will get that same creepy feeling of time standing still. These places look and feel the same as they did when I first fell in love with the ocean, decades ago. I even wrote about this in 2003, when Kenya's tourism industry was reeling from terrorism alerts and travel advisories. I felt the crisis was not external: it was a failure of imagination.

Of course, we have some quite excellent beach resorts in this land (I patronise most of them). These properties offer rooms designed with sun and sea in mind; they provide interesting and varied cuisine; they run a competent and effective operation; and they have motivated their employees to give full expression to their warm African smiles. But these great hotels can be counted on one hand. The rest sit back with dulled imaginations, no better than the beach boys they periodically clear out of their beachfronts.

What do these three phenomena have in common? A collective failure of imagination, of creativity, of innovation, of new possibilities. We are all selling the bleeding obvious. Our tourist industry was once very creative: it spawned floating restaurants, bush breakfasts, balloon safaris, outstanding new cuisines. But then it all stopped. We have become fossilised and petrified, afraid of change and taking few risks.

If Africa, its industries and its people are ever to make meaningful progress, we must learn to go beyond selling what's easy. We have been given beautiful resources which we systematically fail to utilise to their fullest potential. It is no longer enough to be yet another cookie-cutter hotel - you have to add genuine value in terms of service, cuisine and entertainment for the well-travelled tourist who has seen much better in the Maldives and Bali. It is no longer enough to rely on planeloads brought out here on low-cost tours by the same old operators from the same old source markets.

This is a time for re-imagining our coastline and its economy. We must produce products of the mind, not just the body. We must raise our game, once and for all. For a start, we could stop singing 'Malaika'. It was a great melody. But after four decades, it's time for a new song.

June 2008

120

The Kenyan priorities quiz

As Kenya taxis on the runway preparing for take-off, it is important to get a sense of priority. We must all realise what's hot, and what's really not. Otherwise we are going to go round and round this airport and watch all those other planes zooming off into the sky. I have designed a special quiz for Kenyans to test their priorities. Jump right in...

1. **The person best suited to being the President of Kenya is:**

    a. The person who truly understands that a leader's one and only purpose is to improve the life of citizens.

    b. The craftiest and most manipulative member of my tribe.

    c. Me, myself and I - no one else will do.

2. **What is the best way to address the crisis in our schools?**

    a. Through careful thought and resolute action.

    b. By forming a commission of inquiry with 30 eminent persons to report back within 7 years.

    c. By forcing students to wear white tunics, prohibiting groups of more than two, putting bars on their windows and caning them all every morning at 6.00 am.

3. **We have one of the world's highest road mortality rates. How can we bring this down?**

    a. By re-educating the nation on the importance of the highway code and safe driving.

b.   By implementing a crackdown on dangerous driving and imposing punitive penalties.

c.   By ignoring those who overtake at 150 kph on narrow roads while talking on the phone, and arresting those with slightly low pressure in one tyre.

4. **If you were mayor of Nairobi, what would your most pressing priority be?**

a.   To roll out a comprehensive and thoughtful plan to reduce traffic congestion

b.   To arrest the unchecked pollution and environmental degradation that makes Nairobians perpetually sickly

c.   To arrest residents who attempt to trim their own trees and hedges within their own compounds.

5. **How can we raise the business sector in this country to world-class standards?**

a.   By engaging in massive infrastructural development to reduce the cost of doing business, and providing top-notch transport, power and communications.

b.   By creating a series of enterprise funds to ignite the entrepreneurship of the wider population.

c.   By stopping all businesses from displaying signage or making tea in their kitchens.

6. **Who is the country's greatest enemy?**

a.   The leader who plunders the national purse and promotes ethnic hatred.

b. The Kenyan who takes no pride in his work and delivers utter mediocrity day in, day out.

c. Anyone who tries to smoke or have his shoes shined on the street.

7. Which country is our most important trading partner?

a. Any nation that is founded on sound values and engages in ethical and equitable trading practice.

b. Our neighbouring countries, so that we can develop critical mass and form an important economic bloc.

c. Libya.

8. What is the quickest short-cut to success?

a. There is none.

b. A degree that says 'MSc in ICT Studies', procured from River Road.

c. Relatives in high places.

9. Who is responsible for educating your children?

a. I am.

b. Teachers (I think).

c. The maid, the television set and assorted criminal elements in our estate.

10. To whom do you owe allegiance?

a. All upstanding members of the human race

b. My nation.

c. The few dozen people who emerged from the village where my great-grandfather was born, and who speak like me.

Scoring

Award yourself:

1 point for every '**a**' answer,
3 points for every '**b**' answer
5 points for every '**c**' answer

Tot up your total: _____ points.

Evaluation

10 - 15 points
What are you still doing in this country? Dude, you should have packed your bags long ago.

16 - 40 points
You are pragmatic and understand compromise, but still maintain a dangerous idealistic streak. You will not rise very far.

41 - 50 points
Ah, a born Kenyan leader, one of nature's finest creations. Bigoted, deluded, authoritarian and selfish. Get your election campaign into gear immediately - your chances of taking high office look excellent.

August 2008

How peculiar we are

Safaricom CEO Michael Joseph is perplexed again. His company's latest promotion has turned out disastrously. The offer of "free" calls after 9.00 pm every day has clogged the network and proved a nightmare for people trying to make calls at night. Why? Because Kenyans keep piling in in droves to make their calls at precisely 9:00 pm rather than staggering the load.

Mr. Joseph will not want to call us 'peculiar', but I certainly do. We are indeed a most peculiar people who spend our time doing some most peculiar things. For the benefit of businesspeople, visitors and general observers, I would like to provide another "free" service: explaining our top three peculiarities as a nation.

Peculiarity No 1: We go crazy if things are "free"

Mr Joseph will no doubt agree: it's not a good idea to offer free things to Kenyans. They will over-consume it to the point of madness. This has happened with the latest Safaricom offer; it has been happening for years in the company's customer care numbers. Phoning these numbers is free; therefore no-one can ever get through. Why? Because people keep calling several times a day for the silliest of reasons!

This love of "free" things is the reason why, as a business, you can't fail with offers that say 'buy-one-get-one-free'. The second item is, of course, not free - both items are marked down. But who cares? The word 'free' is enough!

The same thing happened with the Safaricom IPO. Small investors seemed to believe they were onto a freebie - double your money overnight, and best of all, a bank will lend you the capital to do it! Many are now nursing their wounds, having sold their trivial allocation for trivial gain or even a loss - but with a bank loan to repay every month.

This love of free things is not just confined to the poor. It afflicts those in high places, too. For all these decades, we have been in love with "free" donor aid. When donors line up to dish out handouts, Kenyan leaders are the first in line. Of course, donor aid is not free at all - begging comes with huge opportunity and psychological costs attached. But hey, it sounds free, so let's get some!

Peculiarity No 2: We don't behave unless we are made to
Wherever you see Kenyans forming an orderly queue, you can rest assured that there is an askari or other figure of authority nearby carrying a large rungu. Kenyans don't form queues unless they are made to do it. Witness what happens in lifts that don't have askaris nearby. Incoming passengers will run in before the outgoing ones have a chance to come out. What sense does that make?

This inability to queue is apparent in our traffic jams everyday. Roads naturally lend themselves to queueing, except in Kenya. Whenever you find yourself in a slow-moving line of cars, just look at your side-view mirror. Within seconds, some imbecile will rush out onto the oncoming lane to overtake the whole line - followed by half-a-dozen other imbeciles. This will cause great consternation to the oncoming vehicles, and unmitigated chaos will ensue - every day. However, where the traffic police are in attendance and dishing out fines, Kenyans will line up patiently and obediently.

Peculiarity No 3: We are professional hypocrites

Everyone is a hypocrite to some extent, but in Kenya we make a career out of it. Anyone observing us would soon conclude that we have many mouths that say many different things. Politicians promise jobs, wealth, land etc with aplomb, in the full knowledge that these things will never be delivered. CEOs talk convincingly about customer focus, people-centredness, etc - but cut customer service and make sweeping layoffs as soon as there is the smell of a market downturn. Many of us claim to be 'above tribe' in mixed company, but crack evil jokes once people from 'the other tribe' have left the scene.

The rich residents of Lake Naivasha used to wax lyrical about "their" beautiful lake and complain incessantly about small fishermen and minor polluters, in years past. These days they have discovered flower farming and now see the lake as a resource to be exploited and contaminated, because there is big money in it. Beauty be damned!

Interestingly, the hypocrisy extends to more recent denizens of our peculiar land. Development partners and foreign embassies are often the loudest critics of environmental degradation. But when it's time to build their headquarters, they will happily mow down acres of virgin forest in Karura - simply so that they have a nice sylvan setting in which to work.

So, there you are: that's us. Well-travelled observers will know, however, that we are no more or less peculiar than anyone else. All societies have their idiosyncrasies, good and bad. The point is to know what they are, laugh about the harmless ones - and do something about the ones that hold us all back.

June 2008

Even more peculiar...

Be in no doubt: we are a most peculiar nation. We are peculiar in our homes, peculiar in our places of work and worship, and peculiar when we meet socially. We are peculiar in how we talk, work and behave. Indeed, the extent of our peculiarities is in itself peculiar.

Here are just six more peculiarities, big and small, based on my common observation, in no particular order. Enjoy!

Peculiarity Number One: our MPs.
Naturally, since peculiar is their collective middle name. Why is it that when these people are at rallies and in their home towns, they always have very angry faces - deep frowns, wild eyes, saliva splattering everywhere as they talk of plots and conspiracies? But when they get together in parliament, sitting side-by-side with the very people they have been raging against, all MPs seem to become jovial, convivial and jocular in the extreme, as though they are meeting old friends? Why are these people laughing? Or could it be that the joke is really on us?

Peculiarity Number Two: many well-to-do Kenyans are members of gyms and fitness clubs, where they go for regular workouts. But please observe any such Kenyans on their way to a session. They will park their cars as close as possible to the entrance, and then take the elevator or escalator to the health club. In other words, they pay big money to get fit, but spurn all opportunities to burn calories that are free of charge. In fact, Kenyans will easily wait five minutes for a lift just to go up one flight of stairs! Is it money we enjoy burning or calories? Or could it be that we join health clubs just to see and be seen?

Peculiarity Number Three: why do we become religious just once a week? Most churches, temples and mosques are packed to the rafters one day in seven, and you would think the gathered brethren would pay at least minor lip service to the requirements of their religions on the remaining days. Not a bit of it! After singing hymns, the rest of the week we engage in corruption, fraud, deceit, adultery and hate speech without batting an eyelid. Why do we imagine that being religious is a one-day thing, a time to spruce yourself up, put on your best pious smile, and pretend to be holy? Or could it be we go there just to see and be seen?

Peculiarity Number Four: why are Kenyan roads recarpeted so frequently? Our peculiarity lies in thinking of this as a good thing. Indeed, many roads in Nairobi have had a fresh layer of tarmac laid on them in recent times, and Nairobians have applauded. But how long does the new layer last? Six to twelve months at most. And so the contractors return like the seasons, busy (usually during rush hour) doing good for the nation. Why do we drive past and accept this? A good road, well constructed with all proper materials going into it, should last thirty to forty years in all weather conditions, and needs only minor maintenance. But that does not suit us here, where we prefer to keep people busy every year. Or could it be that all roads in Kenya just go round in circles?

Peculiarity Number Five: Kenyan drivers of all social classes, it can generally be agreed, drive like uncouth ruffians who care not a jot about anyone else. They engage in asinine acceleration, brainless braking and obtuse overtaking. But only on working days! On Sundays, a rather different Kenyan driver emerges: driving at a gentle constant speed, with no sudden braking, accelerating or overtaking. What gives? Do the good people emerge only on Sundays? Or could it be that they are the same weekday ruffians, but on Sundays they drive their own cars and buy their own petrol, so sensible driving suddenly makes sense?

Peculiarity Number Six: why is it that when a Kenyan wants you to feel sorry for him, he will show you his net pay, after deductions? Even people on rather generous pay packages will invite your sympathy by telling you how little they "take home" every month. Do they imagine that all the money deducted for loans (that they themselves have taken) benefits somebody else? The car you are paying for, the house you are building, the advance you took - are those not yours? Even our MPs, with their world-beating remuneration, asked for pity recently by telling us how little their "take-home" is. Poor things. Those 4WD cars and rural mansions must weigh so heavily on them. Or could it be I am just lacking in sympathy?

So, that's what I find peculiar. What about you? Let us take comfort in the fact that peculiarity afflicts all nations. How else do we explain that the home of Catholicism keeps voting for a bumptious buccaneer, alleged serial philanderer and graceless buffoon called Silvio Berlusconi?

May 2009

Acknowledgements

I am very grateful to two sets of people.

First, the editorial team members at the *Sunday Nation* who have allowed me to pontificate, castigate, vituperate, denigrate and fulminate on their pages for nearly seven years. I have been given great license to roam, and am very grateful for the support given to my peculiar column by the region's greatest newspaper.

Second, to the young and brave people at Storymoja, my publisher, who have taken on the mission of putting a book in every hand. A very peculiar goal in a country notorious for only reading newspapers. Long may their peculiarity flourish.

Fellow writers, we want to see your work

If your manuscript is hot enough to be selected for publication, we will help you edit it, and guarantee you royalties from sales. We may also invite you to attend our writer's workshops, so be sure to include your name, e-mail address, telephone number, and information about yourself. Email your work to:
submissions@storymojaafrica.co.ke

Uta Do? Business Series
Have you started or ran a successful business? This is an opportunity to share what you have learnt along the way with young entrepreneurs. We seek practical insider information, without the jargon, on starting any kind of business in East Africa, or dealing with any particular aspect of business practice. Local examples are a must! If you have a great idea, send us an outline and we may commission you to write the book and guide you along the way. Maximum length: 20,000 words.

Storymoja Business Series
We also seek other business books targeted to those making the corporate sector, taking in consideration the local environment and regulatory conditions, including business success stories, biographies, management books, etc. Maximum length: 40,000 words.

Life Changing Moments
Is there an event in your life that has profoundly affected you? A story of something that made you grow up real fast, or changed the way you do things, or altered the way you work, or influenced how you deal with your family or relationships, or an event that changed your perspective in a positive and meaningful way?

Please share it with us in 2,000 words or less.

Humour
If you have a funny take on life, be it about the dating scene, tribal stereotypes, the gender wars, politics or sports, in fact on any aspect of living in our outrageous, hilarious, wonderful region, please send it in. Maximum length 20,000 words – but it could be in the form of a series of shorter pieces. Make us laugh to tears and we will publish you.

True Crime Stories
Have you been conned? Cheated out of your property by relatives, friends, employees or strangers? Have you been mistreated, unjustly treated, scammed, hijacked, raped, robbed or beaten? Do you know of a scandal at your workplace? Are you the victim or perpetuator of a crime? We are looking for true crime stories and scandalous sagas of up to 20,000 words. We will protect your identity if you chose to remain anonymous. Outrage us and we will publish you.

Children's Stories
Do you see the world like a child does? We seek wacky children's stories set here in East Africa. No stories like "How the Leopard got its Spots." Enough already! We seek fiction and non-fiction that deals with what kids go though now. Read our current titles for inspiration. Categories:

1-4 years	500 words max
5-8 years	2,000 - 4,000 words
8-12 years	6,000 - 12,000 words
12-16 years	20,000 - 60,000 words

Make kids laugh out loud or open their eyes wide with amazement, then send us the manuscript.